TerminusDB
Data Modeling and
Schema Design

Steve Hoberman

Donny Winston

Align > Refine > Design Series

Technics Publications

Published by:

115 Linda Vista, Sedona, AZ 86336 USA
https://www.TechnicsPub.com

Edited by Sadie Hoberman
Cover design by Lorena Molinari

First Printing 2023
Copyright © 2023 by Technics Publications

ISBN, print ed.   9781634623100
ISBN, Kindle ed. 9781634623117
ISBN, ePub ed.   9781634623124
ISBN, PDF ed.   9781634623131

Library of Congress Control Number: 2023933974

Contents

List of Figures

List of Tables

About the Book

My daughter can make a mean brownie. She starts with a store-bought brownie mix and adds chocolate chips, apple cider vinegar, and other "secret" ingredients to make her own unique delicious brownie.

Building a robust database design meeting users' needs requires a similar approach. The store-bought brownie mix represents a proven recipe for success. Likewise, there are data modeling practices that have proven successful over many decades. The chocolate chips and other secret ingredients represent the special additions that lead to an exceptional product. TerminusDB has several special design considerations, much like the chocolate chips. Combining proven data modeling practices with TerminusDB design-specific practices creates a series of data models representing powerful communication tools, greatly improving the opportunities for an exceptional design and application.

In fact, each book in the Align > Refine > Design series covers conceptual, logical, and physical data modeling for a specific database product, combining the best of data modeling practices with solution-specific design considerations. It is a winning combination.

My daughter's first few brownies were not a success, although as the proud (and hungry) dad, I ate them anyway—and they were still tasty. It took practice to get the brownie to come out amazing. We need practice on the modeling side as well. Therefore, each book in the series follows the same animal shelter case study, allowing you to see the modeling techniques applied to reinforce your learning.

If you want to learn how to build multiple database solutions, read all the books in the series. Once you read one, you can pick up the techniques for another database solution even quicker.

Some say my first word was "data". I have been a data modeler for over 30 years and have taught variations of my **Data Modeling Master Class** since 1992—currently up to the 10th Edition! I have written nine books on data modeling, including *The Rosedata Stone* and *Data Modeling Made Simple*. I review data models using my Data Model Scorecard® technique. I am the founder of the Design Challenges group, creator of the Data Modeling Institute's Data Modeling Certification exam, Conference Chair of the Data Modeling Zone conferences, director of Technics Publications, lecturer at Columbia University, and recipient of the Data Administration Management Association (DAMA) International Professional Achievement Award.

Thinking of my daughter's brownie analogy, I have perfected the store-bought brownie recipe. That is, I know how to model. However, I am not an expert in every database solution. That is why each book in this series combines my proven data modeling practices with database solution experts. So, for this book, Donny Winston and I are making the brownie together. I work on the store-bought brownie piece, and Donny works on adding the chocolate chips and other delicious ingredients.

Donny Winston is an independent research data engineer through his company, Polyneme LLC. He makes research organizations more effective by shifting data management practices from a "lumpy", bibliographic model to a fine-grained, query-oriented model. Donny is a TerminusDB enthusiast, and he thanks TerminusDB core team members (in alphabetical order) Sreya Chatterjee, Luke Feeney, Gavin Mendel-Gleason, Matthijs van Otterdijk, Robin de Rooij, and Oliver Smith, as well as fellow enthusiast Philippe Höij, for their support and feedback.

We hope our tag team approach shows you how to model any TerminusDB solution. Particularly for those with experience in data modeling of relational databases, the book provides a bridge from the traditional methods to the very different way we model to leverage the benefits of NoSQL in general and TerminusDB in particular.

Audience

We wrote this book for two audiences:

- Data architects and modelers who wish to expand their modeling skills to include TerminusDB. That is, those of us who know how to make a store-bought brownie but are looking for those secret additions like chocolate chips.

- Database administrators and developers who know TerminusDB but need to expand their modeling skills. That is, those of us who know the value of chocolate chips and other ingredients but need to learn how to combine these ingredients with those store-bought brownie mixes.

This book contains a foundational introduction followed by three approach-driven chapters. Think of the introduction as making that store-built brownie and the subsequent chapters as adding chocolate chips and other yummy ingredients. More on these four sections:

- **Introduction: About Data Models**. This overview covers the three modeling characteristics of precise, minimal, and visual; the three model components of entities, relationships, and attributes; the three model levels of conceptual (align), logical (refine), and physical (design); and the three modeling perspectives of relational, dimensional, and query. By the end of this introduction, you will know data modeling concepts and how to approach any data modeling assignment. This introduction will be useful to database administrators and developers who need a foundation in data modeling, as well as data architects and data modelers who need a modeling refresher.

- **Chapter 1: Align**. This chapter will explain the data modeling align phase. We explain the purpose of aligning our business vocabulary, introduce our animal shelter case study, and then walk through the align approach. This chapter will be useful for both audiences, architects/modelers and database administrators/developers.

- **Chapter 2: Refine**. This chapter will explain the data modeling refine phase. We explain the purpose of refine, refine the model for our animal shelter case study, and then walk through the refine approach. This chapter will be useful for both audiences, architects/modelers and database administrators/developers.

- **Chapter 3: Design**. This chapter will explain the data modeling design phase. We explain the purpose of design, design the model for our animal shelter case study, and then walk through the design approach. This chapter will be useful for both audiences, architects/modelers and database administrators/developers.

We end each chapter with three tips and three takeaways. We aim to write as concisely yet comprehensively as possible to make the most of your time.

Most data models throughout the book were created using Mermaid (https://mermaid.js.org/) and are accessible for reference at https://github.com/polyneme/align-refine-design. Let's begin!

Donny and Steve

About Data Models

This chapter is all about making that store-built brownie. We present the data modeling principles and concepts within a single chapter. In addition to explaining the data model, this chapter covers the three modeling characteristics of precise, minimal, and visual; the three model components of entities, relationships, and attributes; the three model levels of conceptual (align), logical (refine), and physical (design); and the three modeling perspectives of relational, dimensional, and query. By the end of this chapter, you will know how to approach any data modeling assignment.

Data model explanation

A model is a precise representation of a landscape. Precise means there is only one way to read a model—it is neither ambiguous nor up to interpretation. You and I read the same model the exact same way, making the model an extremely valuable communication tool.

We need to 'speak' a language before we can discuss content. That is, once we know how to read the symbols on a model (syntax), we can discuss what the symbols represent (semantics).

Once we understand the syntax, we can discuss the semantics.

For example, a map like the one in Figure 1 helps a visitor navigate a city. Once we know what the symbols mean on a map, such as lines representing streets, we can read the map and use it as a valuable navigation tool for understanding a geographical landscape.

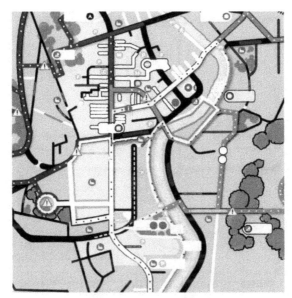

Figure 1: Map of a geographic landscape.

A blueprint like the one in Figure 2 helps an architect communicate building plans. The blueprint, too, contains only representations, such as rectangles for rooms and lines for pipes. Once we know what the rectangles and lines mean on a blueprint, we know what the structure will look like and can understand the architectural landscape.

The data model like the one in Figure 3 helps businesses and technologists discuss requirements and terminology. The data model, too, contains only representations, such as rectangles for terms and lines for business rules. Once we know what the rectangles and lines mean on a data model, we can debate and eventually agree on the business requirements and terminology captured in the informational landscape.

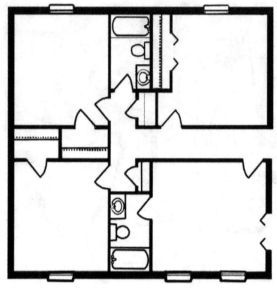

Figure 2: Map of an architectural landscape.

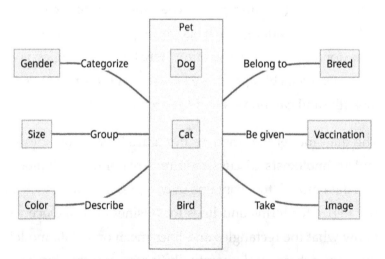

Figure 3: Map of an informational landscape.

A data model is a precise representation of an information landscape. We build data models to confirm and document our understanding of other perspectives.

In addition to precision, two other important characteristics of the model are minimal and visual. Let's discuss all three characteristics.

Three model characteristics

Models are valuable because they are precise—there is only one way to interpret the symbols on the model. We must transform the ambiguity in our verbal and sometimes written communication into a precise language. Precision does not mean complex—we need to keep our language simple and show the minimal amount needed for successful communication. In addition, following the maxim "a picture is worth a thousand words," we need visuals to communicate this precise and simple language for the initiative.

Precise, minimal, and visual are three essential characteristics of the model.

Precise

Bob: How's your course going?

Mary: Going well. But my students are complaining about too much homework. They tell me they have many other classes.

Bob: The attendees in my advanced session say the same thing.

Mary: I wouldn't expect that from graduates. Anyway, how many other offerings are you teaching this semester?

Bob: I'm teaching five offerings this term and one is an evening not-for-credit class.

We can let this conversation continue for a few pages, but do you see the ambiguity caused by this simple dialog?

- What is the difference between **Course, Class, Offering,** and **Session**?
- Are **Semester** and **Term** the same?
- Are **Student** and **Attendee** the same?

Precision means "exactly or sharply defined or stated." Precision means there is only one interpretation for a term, including the term's name, definition, and connections to other terms. Most issues organizations face related to growth, credibility, and saving lives, stem from a lack of precision.

On a recent project, Steve needed to explain data modeling to a group of senior human resource executives. These very high-level managers lead departments responsible for implementing a very expensive global employee expense system. Steve felt the last thing these busy human resource executives needed was a lecture on data modeling. So instead, he asked each of these managers sitting around this large boardroom table to write down their definition of an employee. After a few minutes, most of the writing stopped and he asked them to share their definitions of an employee.

As expected, no two definitions were the same. For example, one manager included contingency workers in his definition, while another included summer interns. Instead of spending the remaining meeting time attempting to come to a consensus on the meaning of an employee, we discussed the reasons we create data models, including the value of precision. Steve explained that after we complete the difficult journey of achieving the agreed-upon employee definition and document it in the form of a data model, no one will ever have to go through the same painful process again. Instead, they can use and build upon the existing model, adding even more value for the organization.

Making terms precise is hard work. We need to transform the ambiguity in our verbal and sometimes written communication into a form where five people can read about the term and each gets a single clear picture of the term, not five different interpretations. For example, a group of business users initially define **Product** as:

Something we produce intending to sell for profit.

Is this definition precise? If you and I read this definition, are we each clear on what *something* means? Is *something* tangible like a hammer or instead some type of service? If it is a hammer and we donate this hammer to a not-for-profit organization, is it still a hammer? After all, we didn't make a *profit* on it. The word *intending* may cover us, but still, shouldn't this word be explained in more detail? And who is *we*? Is it our entire organization or maybe just a subset? What does *profit* really mean anyway? Can two people read the word *profit* and see it very differently?

You see the problem. We need to think like a detective to find gaps and ambiguous statements in the text to make terms precise. After some debate, we update our **Product** definition to:

A product, also known as a finished product, is something that is in a state to be sold to a consumer. It has completed the manufacturing process, contains a wrapper, and is labeled for resale. A product is different than a raw material and a semi-finished good. A raw material such as sugar or milk, and a semi-finished good such as melted chocolate is never sold to a consumer. If in the future, sugar or milk is sold directly to consumers, than sugar and milk become products.

Examples:
Widgets Dark Chocolate 42 oz
Lemonizer 10 oz
Blueberry pickle juice 24 oz

Ask at least five people to see if they are all clear on this particular initiative's definition of a product. The best way to test precision is to try to break the definition. Think of lots of examples and see if everyone makes the same decision as to whether the examples are products or not.

In 1967, G.H. Mealy wrote a whitepaper where he made this statement:

> We do not, it seems, have a very clear and commonly agreed upon set of notions about data—either what they are, how they should be fed and cared for, or their relation to the design of programming languages and operating systems.[1]

Although Mr. Mealy made this claim over 50 years ago, if we replace *programming languages and operating systems* with the word *databases*, we can make a similar claim today.

Aiming for precision can help us better understand our business terms and business requirements.

Minimal

The world around us is full of obstacles that can overwhelm our senses, making it very challenging to focus only on the relevant information needed to make intelligent decisions. Therefore, the model contains a minimal set of symbols and text, simplifying a subset of the real world by only including representations of what we need to understand. Much is filtered out on a model, creating an incomplete but extremely useful reflection of reality. For example, we might need to communicate

---

[1] G. H. Mealy, "Another Look at Data," AFIPS, pp. 525-534, 1967 Proceedings of the Fall Joint Computer Conference, 1967. https://doi.org/10.1145/1465611.1465682.

descriptive information about **Customer**, such as their name, birth date, and email address. But we will not include information on the process of adding or deleting a customer.

Visual

Visual mean that we need a picture instead of lots of text. Presentations using visual aids were found to be 43% more persuasive than unaided presentations.[2]

We might read an entire document but not reach that moment of clarity until we see a figure or picture summarizing everything. Imagine reading directions to navigate from one city to another versus the ease of reading a map that shows visually how the roads connect.

Three model components

The three components of a data model are entities, relationships, and attributes (including keys).

---

[2] Vogel et al., "Persuasion and the Role of Visual Presentation Support: The UM/3M Study." University of Minnesota, June 1986. https://doi.org/20.500.14132/MISRC-WP-86-11.

Entities

An entity is a collection of information about something important to the business. It is a noun considered basic and critical to your audience for a particular initiative. Basic means this entity is mentioned frequently in conversations while discussing the initiative. Critical means the initiative would be very different or non-existent without this entity.

Most entities are easy to identify and include nouns that are common across industries, such as **Customer**, **Employee**, and **Product**. Entities can have different names and meanings within departments, organizations, or industries based on audience and initiative (scope). An airline may call a **Customer** a *Passenger*, a hospital may call a **Customer** a *Patient*, an insurance company may call a **Customer** a *Policyholder*, yet they are all recipients of goods or services.

Each entity fits into one of six categories: who, what, when, where, why, or how. That is, each entity is either a who, what, when, where, why, or how. Table 1 contains a definition of each of these categories, along with examples.

Category	Definition	Examples
Who	Person or organization of interest to the initiative.	Employee, Patient, Player, Suspect, Customer, Vendor, Student, Passenger, Competitor, Author
What	Product or service of interest to the initiative. What the organization makes or provides that keeps it in business.	Product, Service, Raw Material, Finished Good, Course, Song, Photograph, Tax Preparation, Policy, Breed
When	Calendar or time interval of interest to the initiative.	Schedule, Semester, Fiscal Period, Duration
Where	Location of interest to the initiative. Location can refer to actual places as well as electronic places.	Employee Home Address, Distribution Point, Customer Website
Why	Event or transaction of interest to the initiative.	Order, Return, Complaint, Withdrawal, Payment, Trade, Claim
How	Documentation of the event of interest to the initiative. Records events such as a Purchase Order (a "How") recording an Order event (a "Why"). A document provides evidence that an event took place.	Invoice, Contract, Agreement, Purchase Order, Speeding Ticket, Packing Slip, Trade Confirmation

Table 1: Entity categories plus examples.

Entities are traditionally shown as rectangles on a data model, such as these two for our animal shelter:

Pet	Breed

Figure 4: Traditional entities.

Entity instances are the occurrences, examples, or representatives of that entity. The entity **Pet** may have multiple instances, such as Spot, Daisy, and Misty. The entity **Breed** may have multiple instances, such as German Shephard, Greyhound, and Beagle.

Entities and entity instances take on more precise names when discussing specific technologies. For example, entities are tables and instances are rows in a RDBMS like PostgreSQL. Entities are classes and instances are documents in TerminusDB.

Relationships

A relationship represents a business connection between two entities and appears on the model traditionally as a line connecting two rectangles. For example, here is a relationship between **Pet** and **Breed**:

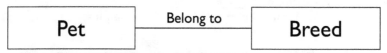

Figure 5: Relationship and label.

The phrase **Belong to** is called a *label*. A label adds meaning to the relationship. Instead of just saying that a

Pet may relate to a **Breed**, we can say that a **Pet** may belong to a **Breed**. **Belong to** is more meaningful than **Relate**.

So far, we know that a relationship represents a business connection between two entities. It would be nice to know more about the relationship, such as whether a **Pet** may belong to more than one **Breed** or whether a **Breed** can categorize more than one **Pet**. Enter cardinality.

Cardinality means the additional symbols on the relationship line that communicate how many instances from one entity participate in the relationship with instances of the other entity.

There are several modeling notations, and each notation has its own set of symbols. Throughout this book, we use a notation called *Information Engineering (IE)*, commonly known as *Crow's foot notation*. The IE notation has been a very popular notation since the early 1980s. If you use a notation other than IE within your organization, you must translate the following symbols into the corresponding symbols in your modeling notation.

We can choose any combination of zero, one, or many for cardinality. *Many* (some people use "more") means one or more. Yes, many includes one. Specifying one or many allows us to capture *how many* of a particular entity instance participate in a given relationship. Specifying zero or one allows us to capture whether an entity instance is or is not required in a relationship.

Recall this relationship between **Pet** and **Breed**:

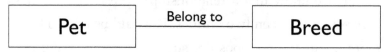

Figure 6: Relationship and label.

Let's now add cardinality.

We first ask the *Participation* questions to learn more. Participation questions tell us whether the relationship is 'one' or 'many'. So, for example:

- Can a **Pet** belong to more than one **Breed**?
- Can a **Breed** categorize more than one **Pet**?

A simple spreadsheet can keep track of these questions and their answers:

Question	Yes	No
Can a Pet belong to more than one Breed?		
Can a Breed categorize more than one Pet?		

We asked the animal shelter experts and received these answers:

Question	Yes	No
Can a Pet belong to more than one Breed?	✓	
Can a Breed categorize more than one Pet?	✓	

We learn that a **Pet** may belong to more than one **Breed**. For example, Daisy is part Beagle and part Terrier. We also learned that a **Breed** may categorize more than one **Pet**. Both Sparky and Spot are Greyhounds.

'Many' (meaning one or more) on a data model in the IE notation is a symbol that looks like a crow's foot (and is called a *crow's foot* by data folks). See Figure 7.

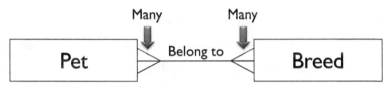

Figure 7: **Displaying the answers to the Participation questions.**

Now we know more about the relationship:

- Each **Pet** may belong to many **Breeds**.
- Each **Breed** may categorize many **Pets**.

We also always use the word 'each' when reading a relationship and start with the entity that makes the most sense to the reader, usually the one with the clearest relationship label.

This relationship is not yet precise, though. So, in addition to asking these two Participation questions, we also need to ask the *Existence* questions. Existence tells us for each relationship whether one entity can exist without the other term. For example:

- Can a **Pet** exist without a **Breed**?
- Can a **Breed** exist without a **Pet**?

We asked the animal shelter experts and received these answers:

Question	Yes	No
Can a Pet exist without a Breed?		✓
Can a Breed exist without a Pet?	✓	

We learn that a **Pet** cannot exist without a **Breed**, and that a **Breed** can exist without a **Pet**. This means, for example, that we may not have any Chihuahuas in our animal shelter. Yet we need to capture a **Breed** (and in this case, one or more **Breeds**), for every **Pet**. As soon as we know about Daisy, we need to identify at least one of her breeds, such as Beagle or Terrier.

Figure 8 displays the answers to these two questions.

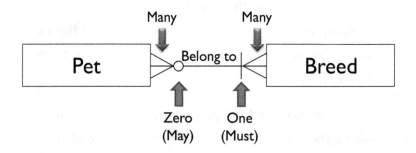

Figure 8: Displaying the answers to the Existence questions.

After adding existence, we have a precise relationship:

- Each **Pet** must belong to many **Breeds**.
- Each **Breed** may categorize many **Pets**.

The Existence questions are also known as the May/Must questions. The Existence questions tell us when reading the relationship, whether we say "may" or "must." A zero means "may", indicating optionality—the entity can exist without the other entity. A **Breed** *may* exist without a **Pet**, for example. A one means "must", indicating required—the entity cannot exist without the other entity. A **Pet** *must* belong to at least one **Breed**, for example.

There are two more questions that need to be asked if we are working on the more detailed logical data model (which will be discussed shortly). These are the *Identification* questions.

Identification tells us for each relationship whether one entity can be identified without the other term. For example:

- Can a **Pet** be identified without a **Breed**?
- Can a **Breed** be identified without a **Pet**?

We asked the animal shelter experts and received these answers:

Question	Yes	No
Can a Pet be identified without a Breed?	✓	
Can a Breed be identified without a Pet?	✓	

We learn that a **Pet** can be identified without knowing a **Breed**. We can identify the pet Sparky without knowing that Sparky is a German Shepherd. In addition, we can identify a **Breed** without knowing the **Pet**. This means, for example, that we can identify the Chihuahua breed without including any information from **Pet**.

A dotted line captures a non-identifying relationship. That is, when the answer to both questions is "yes". A solid line captures an identifying relationship. That is, when one of the answers is "no".

Non-identifying

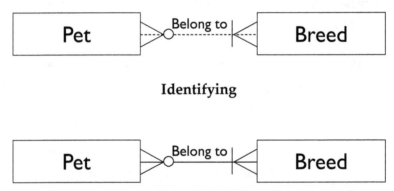

Identifying

Figure 9: A non-identifying (top) and identifying (bottom) relationship.

To summarize, the Participation questions reveal whether each entity has a one or many relationship to the other entity. The Existence questions reveal whether each entity has an optional ("may") or mandatory ("must") relationship to the other entity. The Identification questions reveal whether each entity requires the other entity to bring back a unique entity instance.

Use instances to make things clear in the beginning and eventually help you explain your models to colleagues. See Figure 10 for an example.

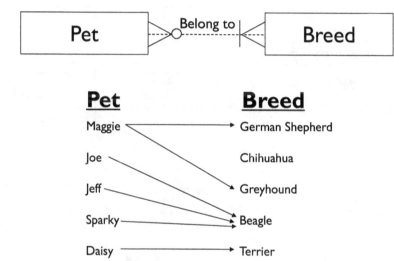

Figure 10: Use sample data to validate a relationship.

You can see from this dataset that a **Pet** can belong to more than one **Breed**, such as Maggie being a German Shepherd/Greyhound mix. You can also see that every **Pet** must belong to at least one **Breed**. We could also have a **Breed** that is not categorizing any **Pets**, such as Chihuahua. In addition, a **Breed** can categorize multiple **Pets**; Joe, Jeff, and Sparky are all Beagles.

Answering all six questions leads to a precise relationship. Precise means we all read the model the same exact way.

Let's say that we have slightly different answers to our six questions:

Question	Yes	No
Can a Pet belong to more than one Breed?		✓
Can a Breed categorize more than one Pet?	✓	
Can a Pet exist without a Breed?		✓
Can a Breed exist without a Pet?	✓	
Can a Pet be identified without a Breed?	✓	
Can a Breed be identified without a Pet?	✓	

These six answers lead to this model:

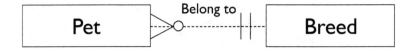

- Each **Pet** must belong to one **Breed**.
- Each **Breed** may categorize many **Pets**.

Figure 11: Different answers to the six questions lead to different cardinality.

On this model, we are only including pure-breed pets, as a **Pet** must be assigned one **Breed**. No mutts in our shelter!

Be very clear on labels. Labels are the verbs that connect our entities (nouns). To read any complete sentence, we need both nouns and verbs. Make sure the labels on the relationship lines are as descriptive as possible. Here are some examples of good labels:

- Contain
- Provide
- Own
- Initiate
- Characterize

Avoid the following words as labels, as they provide no additional information to the reader. You can use these words in combination with other words to make a meaningful label; just avoid using these words by themselves:

- Have
- Associate
- Participate
- Relate
- Are

For example, replace the relationship sentence:

"Each **Pet** must *relate to* one **Breed**."

With:

"Each **Pet** must *belong to* one **Breed**."

Relationships take on more precise names when discussing specific technologies. For example, relationships are constraints in a RDBMS such as PostgreSQL. Relationships are range classes specified using class properties in TerminusDB. However, it is often preferred to implement relationships through embedding as subdocuments. The pros and cons of both approaches are discussed later in the book.

In addition to relationship lines, we can also have a subtyping relationship. The subtyping relationship groups common entities together. For example, the **Dog** and **Cat** entities might be grouped using subtyping under the more generic **Pet** term. In this example, **Pet** would be called the grouping entity or supertype, and **Dog** and **Cat** would be the terms that are grouped together, also known as the subtypes, as shown in Figure 12.

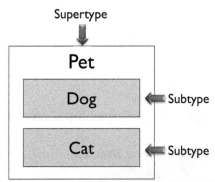

Figure 12: Subtyping is similar to the concept of inheritance.

We would read this model as:

- Each **Pet** may be either a **Dog** or a **Cat**.
- **Dog** is a **Pet**. **Cat** is a **Pet**.

The subtyping relationship means that all of the relationships (and attributes that we'll learn about shortly) that belong to the supertype from other terms also belong to each subtype. Therefore, the relationships to **Pet** also belong to **Dog** and **Cat**. So, for example, cats can be assigned breeds as well, so the relationship to **Breed** can exist at the **Pet** level instead of the **Dog** level, encompassing both cats and dogs. See Figure 13 for an example.

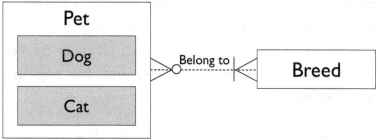

Figure 13: The relationship to Pet is inherited to Dog and Cat.

So, the relationship:

- Each **Pet** must belong to many **Breeds**.
- Each **Breed** may categorize many **Pets**.

Also applies to **Dog** and **Cat**:

- Each **Dog** must belong to many **Breeds**.
- Each **Breed** may categorize many **Dogs**.
- Each **Cat** must belong to many **Breeds**.
- Each **Breed** may categorize many **Cats**.

Not only does subtyping reduce redundancy, but it also makes it easier to communicate similarities across what would appear to be distinct and separate terms. We will discuss later how to achieve this in TerminusDB using the @inherits keyword in class definition.

Attributes (and keys)

An entity contains attributes. An *attribute* is an individual piece of information whose values identify, describe, or measure instances of an entity. The entity **Pet** might contain the attributes **Pet Number** that identifies the **Pet**, **Pet Name** that describes the **Pet**, and **Pet Age** that measures the **Pet**.

Attributes take on more precise names when discussing specific technologies. For example, attributes are columns in a RDBMS such as PostgreSQL. Attributes are properties in TerminusDB.

A candidate key is one or more attributes that uniquely identify an entity instance. We assign an **ISBN** (International Standard Book Number) to every title. The **ISBN** uniquely identifies each title and is, therefore, the title's candidate key. **Tax ID** can be a candidate key for an organization in some countries, such as the United States. **Account Code** can be a candidate key for an account. A **VIN** (Vehicle Identification Number) identifies a vehicle.

A candidate key must be unique and mandatory. Unique means a candidate key value must not identify more than one entity instance (or one real-world thing). Mandatory means a candidate key cannot be empty (also known as *nullable*). Each entity instance must be identified by exactly one candidate key value.

The number of distinct values of a candidate key is always equal to the number of distinct entity instances. If the entity **Title** has **ISBN** as its candidate key, and if there are 500 title instances, there will also be 500 unique ISBNs.

Even though an entity may contain more than one candidate key, we can only select one candidate key to be the primary key for an entity. A primary key is the candidate key that has been chosen to be *the preferred* unique identifier for an entity. An alternate key is a candidate key that, although it has the properties of being unique and mandatory, was not chosen as the primary key though it may still be used to find specific entity instances.

The primary key appears in the entity box with "PK" in parentheses, and the alternate key contains "AK" in parentheses. So, in the following **Pet** entity (Figure 14), **Pet Number** is the primary key and **Pet Name** is the alternate key. Having an alternate key on **Pet Name** means we cannot have two pets with the same name. Whether this can happen or not is a good discussion point. However, the model in its current state would not allow duplicate **Pet Names**.

Pet		
_	_	Pet Number (PK)
_	_	Pet Name (AK)
_	_	Pet Age

Figure 14: An alternate key on Pet Name means we cannot have two pets with the same name. In a Mermaid entity-relationship diagram (erDiagram), entity attributes are expressed as type-name-comment lines, where type is the data type and name is the physical-model name (i.e. without spaces). To emphasize that we are working at the logical refinement level and not at the physical design level, we "stub out" the type and name fields with underscores.

A candidate key can be either simple, compound, or composite. If it is simple, it can be either business or surrogate. Table 2 contains examples of each key type.

	SIMPLE	COMPOUND	COMPOSITE	OVERLOADED
BUSINESS	ISBN	PROMOTION TYPE CODE + PROMOTION START DATE	(CUSTOMER FIRST NAME + CUSTOMER LAST NAME + BIRTHDAY)	STUDENT GRADE
SURROGATE	BOOK ID			

Table 2: Examples of each key type.

Sometimes a single attribute identifies an entity instance, such as **ISBN** for a title. When a single attribute makes up a key, we use the term *simple key*. A simple key can either be a business (also called natural) key or a surrogate key.

A business key is visible to the business (such as **Policy Number** for a **Policy**). A surrogate key is never visible to the business. A surrogate key is created by a technologist to help with a technology issue, such as space efficiency, speed, or integration. It is a unique identifier for a table, often a counter, usually fixed-size, and always system-generated without intelligence, so a surrogate key carries no business meaning. A surrogate key is always *simple*.

Sometimes it takes more than one attribute to uniquely identify an entity instance. For example, both a **Promotion Type Code** and **Promotion Start Date** may be necessary to identify a promotion. When more than one attribute makes up a key, we use the term *compound key*. Therefore, **Promotion Type Code** and **Promotion Start Date** together are a compound candidate key for a promotion. When a key contains more than one piece of information, we use the term *composite key*. A simple key that includes the customer's first name, last name, and birthday, all in the same attribute, would be an example of a simple composite key. When a key contains different attributes, it is called an *overloaded* key. A **Student Grade** attribute might sometimes contain the actual grade, such as A, B, or C. At other times it might just contain a P for Pass and F for Fail. **Student Grade**, therefore, would be an overloaded attribute. **Student Grade** sometimes contains the student's grade, and other times indicates whether the student has passed the class. Let's look at the model in Figure 15:

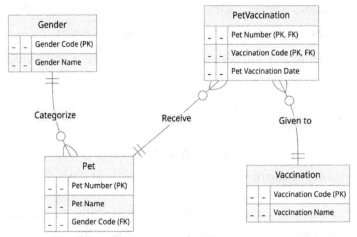

Figure 15: The entity on each "many" side contains a foreign key pointing back to the primary key from the entity on the "one" side.

Here are the rules captured on this model:

- Each **Gender** may categorize many **Pets**.
- Each **Pet** must be categorized by one **Gender**.
- Each **Pet** may Receive many **Vaccinations**.
- Each **Vaccination** may be given to many **Pets**.

The entity on the "one" side of the relationship is called the parent entity, and the entity on the "many" side of the relationship is called the child entity. For example, in the relationship between **Gender** and **Pet**, **Gender** is the parent and **Pet** is the child. When we create a relationship from a parent entity to a child entity, depending on the physical database system used, the parent's primary key may need to be copied as a foreign key to the child. You can see the foreign key, **Gender Code**, in the **Pet** entity.

A foreign key is one or more attributes that link to another entity (or, in a case of a recursive relationship where two instances of the same entity may be related, that is, a relationship that starts and ends with the same entity, a link to the same entity). At the physical level, a foreign key allows a relational database management system to navigate from one table to another. For example, if we need to know the **Gender** of a particular **Pet**, we can use the **Gender Code** foreign key in **Pet** to navigate to the parent **Gender**.

Three model levels

Traditionally, data modeling produces a set of structures for a Relational Database Management System (RDBMS). First, we build the Conceptual Data Model (CDM) (more appropriately called the Business Terms Model or BTM for short) to capture the common business language for the initiative (e.g., "What's a Customer?"). Next, we create the Logical Data Model (LDM) using the BTM's common business language to precisely define the business requirements (e.g., "I need to see the customer's name and address on this report."). Finally, in the Physical Data Model (PDM), we design these business requirements specific for a particular technology such as Oracle, Teradata, or SQL Server (e.g., "Customer Last Name is a variable length not null field with a non-unique index..."). Our PDM represents the RDBMS design for an application. We then generate the Data Definition Language (DDL) from the PDM, which we can run within a RDBMS environment to create the set of tables that will store the application's data. To summarize, we go from common business language to business requirements to design to tables.

Although the conceptual, logical, and physical data models have played a very important role in application development over the last 50 years, they will play an even more important role over the next 50 years.

Regardless of the technology, data complexity, or breadth of requirements, there will always be a need for a diagram that captures the business language (conceptual), the business requirements (logical), and the design (physical).

The names *conceptual*, *logical*, and *physical*, however, are deeply rooted in the RDBMS side. Therefore, we need more encompassing names to accommodate both RDBMS and NoSQL for all three levels.

Align = Conceptual, Refine = Logical, Design = Physical

Using the terms Align, Refine, and Design instead of Conceptual, Logical, and Physical has two benefits: greater purpose and broader context.

Greater purpose means that by rebranding into Align, Refine, and Design, we include what the level does in the name. Align is about agreeing on the common business vocabulary so everyone is *aligned* on terminology and general initiative scope. Refine is about capturing the business requirements. That is, refining our knowledge of the initiative to focus on what is important. Design is about the technical requirements. That is, making sure we accommodate the unique needs of software and hardware on our model.

Broader context means there is more than just the models. When we use terms such as conceptual, most project teams only see the model as the deliverable, and do not recognize all the work that went into producing the model or other related deliverables such as definitions, issue/question resolutions, and lineage (lineage meaning where the data comes from). The align phase includes the conceptual (business terms) model, the refine phase includes the logical model, and the design phase includes the physical model. We don't lose our modeling terms. Instead, we distinguish the model from its broader phase. For example, instead of saying we are in the logical data modeling phase, we say we are in the refine phase, where the logical data model is one of the deliverables. The logical data model exists within the context of the broader refine phase.

However, if you are working with a group of stakeholders who may not warm up to the traditional model names of conceptual, logical, and physical, you can call the conceptual model the *alignment model*, the logical model the *refinement model*, and the physical model the *design model*. Use the terms that would have the largest positive impact on your audience.

The conceptual level is Align, the logical Refine, and the physical Design. Align, Refine, and Design—easy to remember and even rhymes!

Conceptual/Business terms (Align)

We have had many experiences where people who need to speak a common business language do not consistently use the same set of terms. For example, Steve recently facilitated a discussion between a senior business analyst and a senior manager at a large insurance company.

The senior manager expressed his frustration on how a business analyst was slowing down the development of his business analytics application. "The team was meeting with the product owner and business users to complete the user stories on insurance quotes for our upcoming analytics application on quotes, when a business analyst asked the question, *What is a quote?* The rest of the meeting was wasted on trying to answer this question. Why couldn't we just focus on getting the Quote Analytics requirements, which we were in that meeting to do? We are supposed to be Agile!"

If there was a lengthy discussion trying to clarify the meaning of a quote, there is a good chance this insurance company does not understand a quote well. All business users may agree that a quote is an estimate for a policy premium but disagree at what point an estimate becomes a quote. For example, does an estimate have to be based on a certain percentage of facts before it can be considered a quote? How well will Quote Analytics meet the user requirements if the users are not clear as to what a *quote* is? Imagine needing to know the answer to this question:

How many life insurance quotes were written last quarter in the northeast?

Without a common alignment and understanding of *quote*, one user can answer this question based on their definition of *quote*, and someone else can answer based on their different definition of *quote*. One of these users (or possibly both) will most likely get the wrong answer.

Steve worked with a university whose employees could not agree on what a *student* meant, a manufacturing company whose sales and accounting departments differed on the meaning of *return on total assets*, and a financial company whose analysts battled relentlessly over the meaning of a *trade*—it's all the same challenge we need to overcome, isn't it?

It's about working towards a common business language.

A common business language is a prerequisite for success in any initiative. We can capture and communicate the terms underlying business processes and requirements, enabling people with different backgrounds and roles to understand and communicate with each other.

A Conceptual Data Model (CDM), more appropriately called a Business Terms Model (BTM), is a language of symbols and text that simplifies an informational landscape by providing a precise, minimal, and visual tool scoped for a particular initiative and tailored for a particular audience.

This definition includes the need to be well-scoped, precise, minimal, and visual. Knowing the type of visual that will have the greatest effectiveness requires knowing the audience for the model.

The audience includes the people who will validate and use the model. Validate means telling us whether the model is correct or needs adjustments. Use means reading and benefiting from the model. The scope encompasses an initiative, such as an application development project or a business intelligence program.

Knowing the audience and scope helps us decide which terms to model, what the terms mean, how the terms relate to each other, and the most beneficial type of visual. Additionally, knowing the scope ensures we don't "boil the ocean" and model every possible term in the enterprise. Instead, we only focus on those that will add value to our current initiative.

Although this model is traditionally called a *conceptual data model*, the term "conceptual" is often not received as a very positive term by those outside the data field. Therefore, we prefer to call the "conceptual data model" the "business terms model" and will use this term going forward. It is about business terms, and including the term "business" raises its importance as a business-focused deliverable and also aligns with data governance.

A business terms model often fits nicely on a single piece of paper—and not a plotter-size paper! Limiting a BTM to one page is important because it encourages us to select only key terms. We can fit 20 terms on one page but not 500 terms.

Being well-scoped, precise, minimal, and visual, the BTM provides a common business language. As a result, we can capture and communicate complex and encompassing business processes and requirements, enabling people with different backgrounds and roles to initially discuss and debate terms, and to eventually communicate effectively using these terms.

With more and more data being created and used, combined with intense competition, strict regulations, and rapid-spread social media, the financial, liability, and credibility stakes have never been higher. Therefore, the need for a common business language has never been greater. For example, Figure 16 contains a BTM diagram for our animal shelter.

Each of these entities will have a precise and clear definition. For example, **Pet** might have a similar definition to what appears in Wikipedia:

A pet, or companion animal, is an animal kept primarily for a person's company or entertainment rather than as a working animal, livestock, or a laboratory animal.

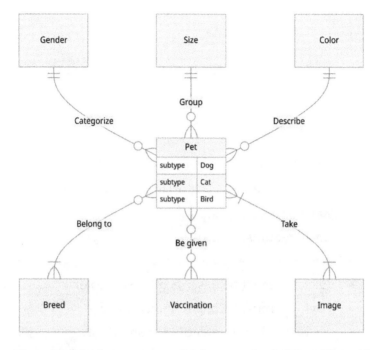

Figure 16: A business terms model for our animal shelter. Mermaid entity-relationship (ER) diagrams, unlike flowchart diagrams, do not support subgraphs. Here, we use ER diagram attributes to designate our Pet subtypes.

More than likely, though, there will be something about the definition that provides more meaning to the reader of a particular data model and is more specific to a particular initiative, such as:

A pet is a dog, cat, or bird that has passed all the exams required to secure adoption. For example, if Sparky has passed all his physical and behavioral exams, we would consider Sparky a pet. However, if Sparky has failed at least one exam, we will label Sparky an animal that we will reevaluate later.

Let's now walk through the relationships depicted in Figure 16:

- Each Pet may be either a Dog, Cat, or Bird.
- Dog is a Pet.
- Cat is a Pet.
- Bird is a Pet.
- Each Gender may categorize many Pets.
- Each Pet must be categorized by one Gender.
- Each Size may group many Pets.
- Each Pet must be grouped by one Size.
- Each Color may describe many Pets.
- Each Pet must be described by one Color.
- Each Pet must belong to many Breeds.
- Each Breed may categorize many Pets.
- Each Pet may be given many Vaccinations.
- Each Vaccination may be given to many Pets.
- Each Pet must take many Images.
- Each Image must be taken of many Pets.

Logical (Refine)

A logical data model (LDM) is a business solution to a business problem. It is how the modeler refines the business requirements without complicating the model with implementation concerns such as software and hardware. For example, after capturing the common business language for a new order application on a BTM, the LDM will refine this model with attributes and more detailed relationships and entities to capture the requirements for this order application. The BTM would contain definitions for **Order** and **Customer**, and the LDM would contain the **Order** and **Customer** attributes needed to deliver the requirements.

Returning to our animal shelter example, Figure 17 contains a subset of the logical data model for our animal shelter.

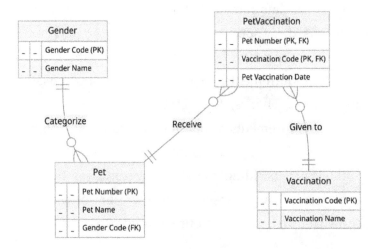

Figure 17: Logical data model subset for our animal shelter.

The requirements for our shelter application appear on this model. This model shows the attributes and relationships needed to deliver a solution to the business. For example, in the **Pet** entity, each **Pet** is identified by a **Pet Number** and described by its name and gender. **Gender** and

Vaccination are defined lists. We also capture that a **Pet** must have one **Gender** and can receive any number (including zero) of **Vaccinations**. Note that an LDM in the context of relational databases respects the rules of normalization. Hence, in the above diagram, associative entities prepare for the physical implementation of many-to-many relationships.

Physical (Design)

The physical data model (PDM) is the logical data model compromised for specific software or hardware. The BTM captures our common business vocabulary, the LDM our business requirements, and the PDM our technical requirements. That is, the PDM is a data model of our business requirements structured to work well with our technology. The physical model represents the technical design. While building the PDM, we address the issues that have to do with specific hardware or software, such as, how can we best design our structures to:

- Process this operational data as quickly as possible?
- Make this information secure?
- Answer these business questions with a sub-second response?

For example, Figure 18 contains a relational version and Figure 19 a nested version of a subset of the physical data model for our animal shelter:

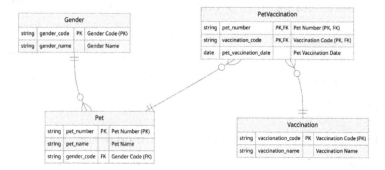

Figure 18: Relational physical data models for our animal shelter.

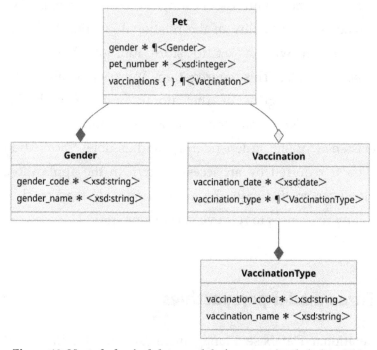

Figure 19: Nested physical data models for our animal shelter. This
diagram uses Mermaid's class-diagram mode. "¶" indicates a
reference rather than an embedding. " {} " indicates a Set collection.
A filled-in diamond signifies composition, and an open diamond
signifies aggregation. "✳" indicates the attribute is required.

We have compromised our logical model to work with specific technology. For example, if we are implementing in a RDBMS such as Oracle, we might need to combine (denormalize) structures together to make retrieval performance acceptable.

Figure 18 is a normalized RDBMS model and Figure 19 shows one possible design to leverage the document approach of TerminusDB. Information belonging together stays together with the nesting of subdocuments. We replace the cardinality of the relational junction table Pet Vaccination with a set to store multiple Vaccination subdocuments. This aggregation approach enables the referential integrity of the atomic unit of each Pet document. Note that the nesting does not prevent the existence of an independently addressable Vaccination class if required by an access pattern in the application. However, in this case, the application code may need to follow references to retrieve vaccination info.

Three model perspectives

Relational Database Management System (RDBMS) and NoSQL are the two main modeling perspectives. Within the RDBMS, the two settings are relational and dimensional. Within NoSQL, the one setting is query. Therefore, the three modeling perspectives are relational, dimensional, and query. Table 3 contrasts relational, dimensional, and query. In this section, we will go into more detail into each of these perspectives.

Factor	Relational	Dimensional	Query
Benefit	Precisely representing data through sets	Precisely representing how data will be analyzed	Precisely representing how data will be received and accessed
Focus	Business rules *constraining* a business process	Business questions *analyzing* a business process	Access paths *providing insights* into a business process
Use case	Operational (OLTP)	Analytics (OLAP)	Discovery
Parent perspective	RDBMS	RDBMS	NoSQL
Example	A Customer must own at least one Account.	How much revenue did we generate in fees by Date, Region, and Product? Also want to see by Month and Year...	Which customers own a checking account that generated over $10,000 in fees this year, own at least one cat, and live within 500 miles of New York City?

Table 3: Comparing relational, dimensional, and query.

A RDBMS stores data in sets based on Ted Codd's groundbreaking whitepapers written from 1969 through 1974. Codd's ideas were implemented in the RDBMS with tables (entities at the physical level) containing attributes. Each table has a primary key and foreign key constraints to enforce the relationships between tables. The RDBMS has been around for so many years primarily because of its ability to retain data integrity by enforcing rules that maintain high-quality data. Secondly, the RDBMS enables efficiency in storing data, reducing redundancy, and saving storage space at the cost of using more CPU power. Over the last decade, the benefit of saving space has diminished as disks get cheaper while CPU performance is not improving. Both trajectories favor NoSQL databases these days.

NoSQL means "NoRDBMS". A NoSQL database stores data differently than a RDBMS. A RDBMS stores data in tables (sets) of arbitrary but fixed arity per table. That is, the various tables can have different numbers of columns, but the number of columns is fixed for all rows of a given table, and where primary and foreign keys drive data integrity and navigation. A NoSQL database does not store data in fixed-arity (N-tuple) sets. For example, TerminusDB stores data as graphs of (transaction) commits of Resource Description Framework (RDF) triples. Other NoSQL solutions may store data in Extensible Markup

Language (XML), JavaScript Object Notation (JSON), or other formats.

Relational, dimensional, and query can exist at all three model levels, giving us nine different types of models, as shown in Table 4. We discussed the three levels of Align, Refine, and Design in the previous section. We align on a common business language, refine our business requirements, and then design our database. For example, if we are modeling a new claims application for an insurance company, we might create a relational model capturing the business rules within the claims process. The BTM would capture the claims business vocabulary, the LDM would capture the claims business requirements, and the PDM would capture the claims database design.

	RELATIONAL	DIMENSIONAL	NoSQL
BUSINESS TERMS (ALIGN)	TERMS AND RULES	TERMS AND PATHS	TERMS AND QUERIES
LOGICAL (REFINE)	SETS	MEASURES WITH CONTEXT	QUERY-FOCUSED HIERACHY
PHYSICAL (DESIGN)	COMPROMISED SETS	STAR SCHEMA OR SNOWFLAKE	ENHANCED HIERACHY

Table 4: Nine different types of models.

Relational

Relational models work best when there is a requirement to capture and enforce business rules. For example, a relational model may be ideal if an operational application requires applying many business rules, such as an order application ensuring that every order line belongs to one and only one order, and that each order line is identified by its order number plus a sequence number. The relational perspective focuses on business rules.

We can build a relational model at all three levels: business terms, logical, and physical. The relational business terms model contains the common business language for a particular initiative. Relationships capture the business rules between these terms. The relational logical data model includes entities along with their definitions, relationships, and attributes. The relational physical data model includes physical structures such as tables, columns, and constraints. The business terms, logical, and physical data models shared earlier are examples of relational. See Figure 20, Figure 21, and Figure 22.

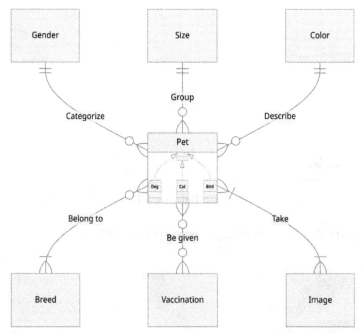

Figure 20: Relational BTM. Mermaid entity-relationship diagrams, unlike flowchart diagrams, do not support subgraphs. Here, we copy-paste a Mermaid class diagram with inheritance arrows to designate our Pet subtypes.

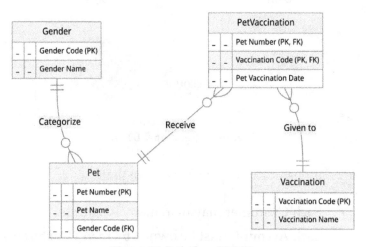

Figure 21: Relational LDM.

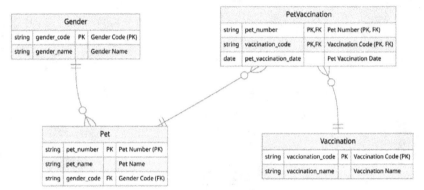

Figure 22: Relational PDM.

Figure 23 contains another example of a BTM.

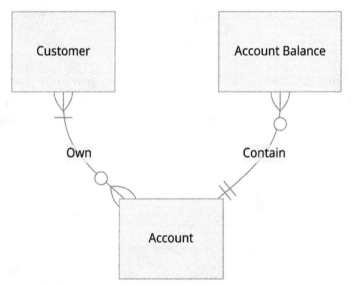

Figure 23: Relational BTM.

The relationships in Figure 23 capture that:

- Each **Customer** may own many **Accounts**.
- Each **Account** must be owned by many **Customers**.

- Each **Account** may contain many **Account Balances**.
- Each **Account Balance** must belong to one **Account**.

We wrote the following definitions during one of our meetings with the project sponsor:

Customer	A customer is a person or organization who has opened one or more accounts with our bank. If members of a household each have their own account, each member of a household is considered a distinct customer. If someone has opened an account and then closed it, they are still considered a customer.
Account	An account is a contractual arrangement by which our bank holds funds on behalf of a customer.
Account Balance	An account balance is a financial record of how much money a customer has in a particular account with our bank at the end of a given time period, such as someone's checking account balance at the end of a month.

For the relational logical data model, we assign attributes to entities (sets) using a set of rules called *normalization*.

Although normalization has a foundation in mathematics (set theory and predicate calculus), we see it more as a technique to design a flexible structure. More specifically, we define normalization as a process of asking business questions, increasing your knowledge of the business and enabling you to build flexible structures that support high-quality data.

The business questions are organized around levels, including First Normal Form (1NF), Second Normal Form (2NF), and Third Normal Form (3NF). These three levels have been neatly summarized by William Kent:

Every attribute depends upon the key, the whole key, and nothing but the key, so help me Codd.

"Every attribute depends upon the key" is 1NF, "the whole key" is 2NF, and "nothing but the key" is 3NF. Note that the higher levels of normalization include the lower levels, so 2NF includes 1NF, and 3NF includes 2NF and 1NF.

To make sure that every attribute depends upon the key (1NF), we need to make sure for a given primary key value, we get at most one value back from each attribute. For example, **Author Name** assigned to a **Book** entity would violate 1NF because for a given book, such as this book, we can have more than author. Therefore, **Author Name** does not belong to the **Book** set (entity) and needs to be moved to a different entity. More than likely, **Author Name** will be assigned to the **Author** entity, and a relationship will exist between **Book** and **Author,** stating among other things, that a **Book** can be written by more than one **Author.**

To make sure every attribute depends upon the whole key (2NF), we need to make sure we have the minimal primary key. For example, if the primary key for **Book** was both **ISBN** and a **Book Title**, we would quickly learn that **Book Title** is not necessary to have in the primary key. An attribute such as **Book Price** would depend directly on the **ISBN,** and therefore including **Book Title** in the primary key would not add any value.

To make sure there are no hidden dependencies ("nothing but the key," which is 3NF), we need to make sure every attribute depends directly on the primary key and nothing else. For example, the attribute **Order Gross Amount** does not depend directly on the primary key of **Order** (most likely, **Order Number**). Instead, **Order Gross Amount** depends upon **List Price** and **Item Quantity,** which are used to derive the **Order Gross Amount.**

Data Modeling Made Simple, by Steve Hoberman, dives into each normalization level, including the levels above 3NF. Realize the main purpose of normalization is to correctly organize attributes into sets. Also, note that the normalized model is built according to the properties of the data and not built according to how the data is being used.

Dimensional models are built to answer specific business questions with ease, and NoSQL models are built to answer queries and identify patterns with ease. The relational model is the only model focused on the intrinsic properties of the data and not usage.

Dimensional

A dimensional data model captures the business *questions* behind one or more business processes. The answers to the questions are metrics, such as **Gross Sales Amount** and **Customer Count**.

A dimensional model is a data model whose only purpose is to allow efficient and user-friendly filtering, sorting, and summing of measures – that is, analytics applications. The relationships on a dimensional model represent navigation paths instead of business rules, as with the relational model. The scope of a dimensional model is a collection of related measures plus context that together address some business process. We build dimensional models based upon one or more business questions that evaluate a business process. We parse the business questions into measures and ways of looking at these measures to create the model.

For example, suppose we work for a bank and would like to better understand the fee generation process. In that case, we might ask the business question, "What is the total amount of fees received by **Account Type** (such as Checking or Savings), **Month, Customer Category** (such as Individual or Corporate), and **Branch**?" See Figure 24. This model also communicates the requirement to see fees not just at a **Month** level but also at a **Year** level, and not just at a **Branch** level, but also at a **Region** and **District** level.

Figure 24: A dimensional BTM for a bank.

Term definitions:

Fee Generation	Fee generation is the business process where money is charged to customers for the privilege to conduct transactions against their account, or money charged based on time intervals, such as monthly charges to keep a checking account open that has a low balance.

Branch	A branch is a physical location open for business. Customers visit branches to conduct transactions.
Region	A region is our bank's own definition of dividing a country into smaller pieces for branch assignment or reporting purposes.
District	A district is a grouping of regions used for organizational assignments or reporting purposes. Districts can and often do cross country boundaries, such as North America and Europe districts.
Customer Category	A customer category is a grouping of one or more customers for reporting or organizational purposes. Examples of customer categories are Individual, Corporate, and Joint.
Account Type	An account type is a grouping of one or more accounts for reporting or organizational purposes. Examples of account types are Checking, Savings, and Brokerage.
Year	A year is a period of time containing 365 days, consistent with the Gregorian calendar.
Month	A month is each of the twelve named periods into which a year is divided.

You might encounter terms such as **Year** and **Month** which are commonly understood terms, and therefore minimal time can be invested in writing a definition. Make sure, though, that these are commonly understood terms, as sometimes even **Year** can have multiple meanings, such as whether the reference is to a fiscal or standard calendar.

Fee Generation is an example of a meter. A meter represents the business process that we need to measure. The meter is so important to the dimensional model that the name of the meter is often the name of the application: for example, the **Sales** meter of a Sales Analytics Application. **District, Region,** and **Branch** represent the levels of detail we can navigate within the **Organization** dimension. A *dimension* is a subject whose purpose is to add meaning to the measures. For example, **Year** and **Month** represent the levels of detail we can navigate within the **Calendar** dimension. So, this model contains four dimensions: **Organization, Calendar, Customer,** and **Account.**

Suppose an organization builds an analytical application to answer questions on how a business process is performing, such as a sales analytics application. Business questions become very important in this case, so we build a dimensional data model. The dimensional perspective focuses on business questions. We can build a dimensional data model at all three levels: business terms, logical, and physical. Figure 24 displayed our business terms model, Figure 25 shows the logical, and Figure 26 the physical.

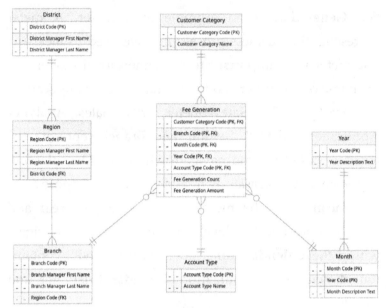

Figure 25: A dimensional LDM for a bank.

Query

Suppose an organization builds an application to discover something new about a business process, such as a fraud detection application. Queries become very important in that case, so we build a query data model.

We can build a query data model at all three levels: business terms, logical, and physical. Figure 27 contains a query business terms model, Figure 28 and Figure 29 the query logical data models, and Figure 30 the query physical data model.

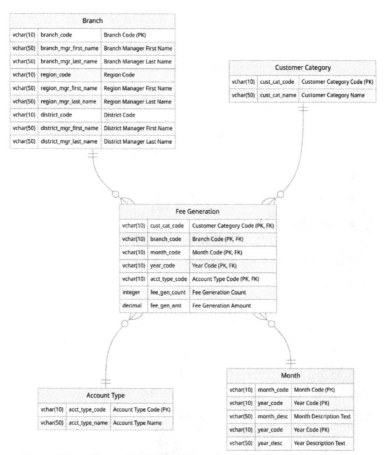

Figure 26: A dimensional PDM for a bank. "vchar" is a character-string field with variable but fixed-maximum length.

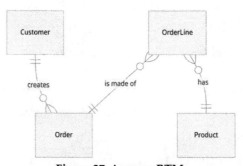

Figure 27: A query BTM.

The Query BTM does not look any different from other BTMs as the vocabulary and scope are the same, independent of the physical database implementation. In fact, we can even ask the Participation and Existence questions for each relationship in our query BTM, if we feel that it would add value. In the above example:

- a **Customer** creates an **Order**
- an **Order** is made of **Order Lines**
- an **Order Line** has a **Product**

It is possible to toggle the display of attributes for the different entities.

When it comes to the logical model, however, access patterns and workload analysis dictate the model. Depending on whether there are queries for maintenance screens for Customers and Products, you could have the strictly embedded logical model in Figure 28, or the model in Figure 29.

The first logical model would lead to a single top-level document class in TerminusDB. It would then be normalized into three tables when instantiated into a physical model for a relational database.

The second logical model will lead to three top-level document classes in TerminusDB to accommodate the maintenance of **Customers** and **Products** independently, while keeping the **Order** class as an aggregate.

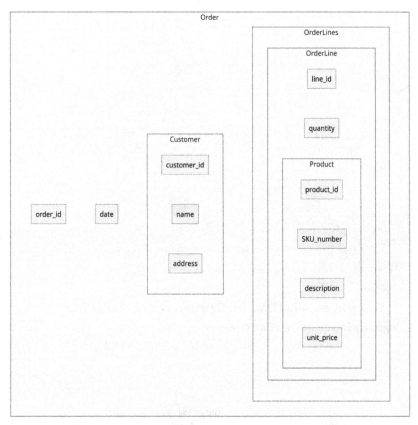

Figure 28: Strictly embedded logical model. Diagrammed as a Mermaid flowchart using subgraphs.

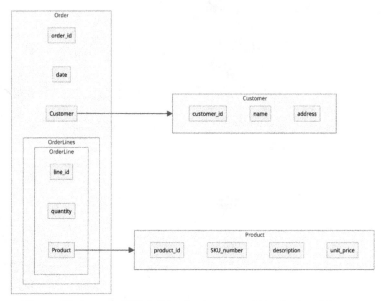

Figure 29: A query LDM. The Customer and Product entities are logically independent of an Order entity with regard to data lifecycle, rather than strictly embedded within an Order.

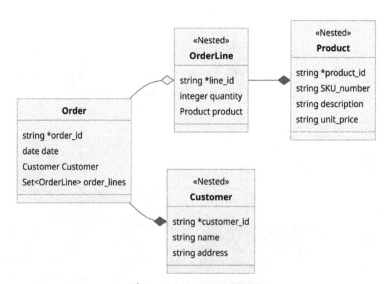

Figure 30: A query PDM.

In the physical model of Figure 30, we show nesting, denormalization, and referencing. Nesting allows aggregating information that belongs together in a user-friendly structure to make it easily understandable by humans. We implement denormalization so a query to retrieve an order would fetch all the necessary information in a single seek without executing expensive joins, even if it is a repetition of the data in the Customer and Product master collections. With TerminusDB, as we'll see later, no physical denormalization is needed to facilitate single-seek logic, as joins are optimized to be inexpensive for RDF triples through covering indexes.

Access patterns might still be required to view and update Customer and Product information regardless of the orders to which they might be linked. Therefore, we can keep the Customer and the Product classes as top-level document classes instead of subdocument classes. In the Order class, we would keep a reference to these other classes through class-ranged properties, and we can lean on the cross-document referential integrity built into the TerminusDB database engine.

Note that there could be a good reason not to update a denormalized piece of information. For example, we should not update the ship-to address of an already fulfilled order because a customer moves to a new address. Only update pending orders. Since denormalization is sometimes more precise than cascading updates, it's not really denormalization, is it?

CHAPTER 1

Align

The his chapter will explain the data modeling align phase. We explain the purpose of aligning our business vocabulary, introduce our animal shelter case study, and then walk through the align approach. We end this chapter with three tips and three takeaways.

Purpose

The align stage aims to capture a common business vocabulary within a business terms model for a particular initiative.

For NoSQL models, you might use a different term than a business terms model, such as a *query alignment model*. We also like this term, which is more specific to the purpose of a NoSQL BTM, as our goal is modeling the queries.

Our animal shelter

A small animal shelter needs our help. They currently advertise their ready-to-adopt pets on their own website. They use a Microsoft Access relational database to keep track of their animals, and they publish this data weekly on their website. See Figure 31 for their current process.

A Microsoft Access record is created for each animal after the animal passes a series of intake tests and is deemed ready for adoption. The animal is called a pet once they are ready for adoption.

Once a week, the pet records are updated on the shelter's website. New pets are added and adopted pets are removed. Not many people know about this shelter, and, therefore, animals often remain unadopted for much longer than the national average. Consequently, they would like to partner with a group of animal shelters to form a consortium where all the shelters' pet information will appear on a much more popular website. Our shelter will need to extract data from its current MS Access database and send it to the consortium database in JSON format. The consortium will then load these JSON feeds into their TerminusDB database with a web front end.

Figure 31: Animal shelter current architecture.

Let's now look at the shelter's current models. The animal shelter built the business terms model (BTM) diagram in Figure 32 to capture the common business language for the initiative.

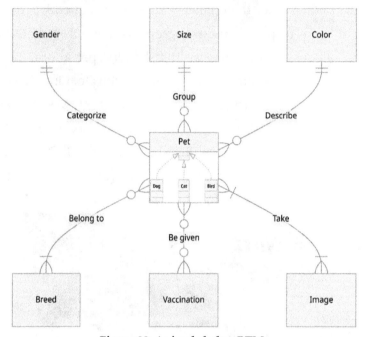

Figure 32: Animal shelter BTM.

In addition to this diagram, the BTM also contains precise definitions for each term, such as this definition of **Pet** mentioned earlier:

A pet is a dog, cat, or bird that has passed all the exams required to secure adoption. For example, if Sparky has passed all his physical and behavioral exams, we would consider Sparky a pet. However, if Sparky has failed at least one exam, we will label Sparky an animal that we will reevaluate later.

Our animal shelter knows its world well and has built fairly solid models. Recall they will send a subset of their data to a consortium via JSON, which the consortium's

TerminusDB database will receive and load for display on their website. Let's go through the align, refine, and design approach for the consortium, and then work on the JSON structure required to move the shelter's data from Microsoft Access to TerminusDB.

Approach

The align stage is about developing the initiative's common business vocabulary. We will follow the steps shown in Figure 33.

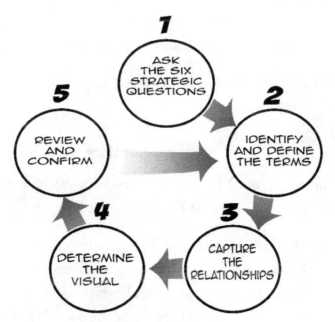

Figure 33: Steps to create a BTM.

Before you begin any project, we must ask six strategic questions (Step 1). These questions are a prerequisite to the success of any initiative because they ensure we choose the right terms for our BTM. Next, identify all terms within the scope of the initiative (Step 2). Make sure each term is clearly and completely defined. Then determine how these terms are related to each other (Step 3). Often, you will need to go back to Step 2 at this point because in capturing relationships, you may come up with new terms. Next, determine the most beneficial visual for your audience (Step 4). Consider the visual that would resonate best with those that will need to review and use your BTM. As a final step, seek approval of your BTM (Step 5). Often at this point, there are additional changes to the model, and we cycle through these steps until the model is accepted.

Let's build a BTM following these five steps.

Step 1: Ask the six strategic questions

Six questions must be asked to ensure a valuable BTM. These questions appear in Figure 34.

1. **What is our initiative?** This question ensures we know enough about the initiative to determine the scope. Knowing the scope allows us to decide which terms should appear on the initiative's BTM. Eric Evans, in his book *Domain-Driven Design*,

introduces the concept of "Bounded Context," which is all about understanding and defining your scope. For example, terms such as **Animal, Shelter Employee**, and **Pet Food** are out of scope.

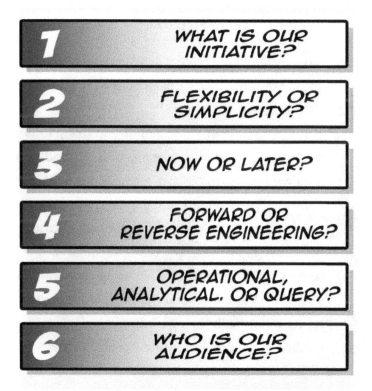

Figure 34: Six questions to ensure model success.

2. **Flexibility or simplicity?** This question ensures we introduce generic terms only if there is a need for flexibility. Generic terms allow us to accommodate new types of terms that we do not know about today and allow us to better group similar terms together. For example, **Person** is flexible, and

Employee is simple. **Person** can include other terms we have not yet considered, such as **Adopter, Veterinarian,** and **Volunteer**. However, **Person** can be a more difficult term to relate to than **Employee.** We often describe our processes using business-specific terms like **Employee.**

3. **Now or later?** This question ensures we have chosen the correct time perspective for our BTM. BTMs capture a common business language at a point in time. If we are intent on capturing how business processes work or are analyzed today, then we need to make sure terms, along with their definitions and relationships, reflect a current perspective (now). If we are intent on capturing how business processes work or are analyzed at some point in the future, such as one year or three years into the future, then we need to make sure terms, along with their definitions and relationships, reflect a future perspective (later).

4. **Forward or reverse engineering?** This question ensures we select the most appropriate "language" for the BTM. If business requirements drive the initiative, then it is a forward engineering effort and we choose a business language. It does not matter whether the organization is using SAP or Siebel, the BTM will contain business terms. If an application is driving the initiative, then it is a

reverse engineering effort, and we choose an application language. If the application uses the term **Object** for the term **Product**, it will appear as **Object** on the model and be defined according to how the application defines the term, not how the business defines the term. As another example of reverse engineering, you might have as your starting point some type of physical data structure, such as a database layout or an XML or JSON document. For example, the following JSON snippet might reveal the importance of **Shelter Volunteer** as a business term:

```
{
    "name": "John Smith",
    "age": 35,
    "address": {
        "street": "123 Main St",
        "city": "Anytown",
        "state": "CA",
        "zip": "12345"
    }
}
```

5. **Operational, analytics, or query?** This question ensures we choose the right type of BTM— relational, dimensional, or query. Each initiative requires its respective BTM.

6. **Who is our audience?** We need to know who will review our model (validator) and who will use our model going forward (users).

1. What is our initiative?

Mary is the animal shelter volunteer responsible for intake. Intake is the process of receiving an animal and preparing the animal for adoption. She has been a volunteer for over ten years and was the main business resource in building the original Microsoft Access database.

She is enthusiastic about the new initiative, seeing it as a way to get animals adopted in less time. We might start off by interviewing Mary, where the goal is to have a clear understanding of the initiative, including its scope:

> **You**: Thanks for making time to meet with me. This is just our first meeting, and I don't want to keep you behind our allocated time, so let's get right to the purpose of our interview and then a few questions. The earlier we identify our scope and then define the terms within this scope, the greater the chance for success. Can you please share with me more about this initiative?

> **Mary**: Sure! The main driver for our initiative is to make our furry friends get adopted faster. Today on average, our pets are adopted in two weeks. We and other small local shelters would like to get this down to five days on average. Maybe even less. We will send our pet data to a consortium we have formed with other local shelters to centralize our listings and reach a wider audience.

> **You**: Do you have all types of pets, or just dogs and cats?

Mary: I'm not sure what kinds of pets the other shelters have other than dogs and cats, but we also have birds up for adoption.

You: Ok, and are there any pets to exclude from this initiative?

Mary: Well, it takes a few days for an animal to be assessed to be considered ready for adoption. We run some tests and sometimes procedures. I like to use the term pet when an animal has completed these processes and is now ready for adoption. So, we do have animals that are not yet pets. We are only including pets in this initiative.

You: Got it. And when somebody is looking for a furry best friend, what kinds of filters would they use?

Mary: I've talked with volunteers at the other shelters too. We feel after filtering first on the type of pet, such as dog, cat, or bird, filtering by breed, gender, color, and size would be the most important filters.

You: What kinds of information would someone expect to see when clicking on a pet description that was returned by the filter selections?

Mary: Lots of images, a cute name, maybe information on the pet's color or breed. That sort of thing.

You: Makes sense. What about people? Do you care about people as part of this initiative?

Mary: What do you mean?

You: Well, the people who drop off pets and the people who adopt pets.

Mary: Yes, yes. We keep track of this information. By the way, the people who drop off animals we call surrenderers, and the people who adopt pets are adopters. We are not sending any personal details to the consortium. We don't see it as relevant and don't want to risk getting sued over privacy issues. Spot the dog will never sue us, but Bob the surrenderer might.

You: I can understand that. Well, I think I understand the scope of the initiative, thank you.

We now have a good understanding of the scope of the initiative. It includes all pets (not all animals) and no people. As we refine the terminology, we might have more questions for Mary around scope.

2. Flexibility or simplicity?

Let's continue the interview to answer the next question.

You: Flexibility or simplicity?

Mary: I don't understand the question.

You: We need to determine whether to use generic terms or, for lack of a better word, more concrete terms. Using generic terms, such as mammal instead of **dog** or **cat**, allows us to accommodate future terms later, such as other kinds of mammals like monkeys or whales.

Mary: We haven't had many whales up for adoption this month. [laughs]

You: Ha!

Mary: Flexibility sounds appealing, but we shouldn't go overboard. I can see eventually we might have other kinds of pets, so a certain level of flexibility would be useful here. But not too much. I remember working on the Microsoft Access system and someone was trying to get us to use a Party concept to capture dogs and cats. It was too hard for us to get our heads around it. Too fuzzy, if you know what I mean.

You: I do know what you mean. Ok, a little flexibility to accommodate different kinds of pets, but not to go overboard. Got it.

3. Now or later?

Now on to the next question.

You: Should our model reflect how things are now at the shelter or how you would like it to be after the consortium's application is live?

Mary: I don't think it matters. We are not changing anything with the new system. A pet is a pet.

You: Ok, that makes things easy.

As we can see from our conversations on these first three questions, getting to the answers is rarely straightforward and easy. However, it is much more efficient to ask them at the beginning of the initiative instead of making assumptions early on and having to perform rework later, when changes are time-consuming and expensive.

4. Forward or reverse engineering?

Since we first need to understand how the business works before implementing a software solution, this is a forward engineering project, and we will choose the forward engineering option. This means driven by requirements and, therefore, our terms will be business terms instead of application terms.

5. Operational, analytics, or query?

Since this initiative is about displaying pet information to drive pet adoption, which is query, we will build a query BTM.

6. Who is our audience?

That is, who is going to validate the model and who is going to use it going forward? Mary seems like the best candidate to be the validator. She knows the existing application and processes very well and is vested in ensuring the new initiative succeeds. Potential adopters will be the users of the system.

Step 2: Identify and define the terms

We first focus on the user stories, then determine the detailed queries for each story, and finally sequence these queries in the order they occur. It can be iterative. For example, we might identify the sequence between two queries and realize that a query in the middle is missing that will require modifying or adding a user story. Let's go through each of these three steps.

1. Write user stories

User stories have been around for a long time and are extremely useful for NoSQL modeling. Wikipedia defines a user story as: *...an informal, natural language description of features of a software system.*

The user story provides the scope and overview for the BTM, also known as a query alignment model. A query alignment model accommodates one or more user stories. The purpose of a user story is to capture at a very high level how an initiative will deliver business value. User stories take the structure of the template in Figure 35.

TEMPLATE	COVERS
AS A (STAKEHOLDER)	WHO?
I WANT TO (REQUIREMENT)	WHAT?
SO THAT (MOTIVATION)	WHY?

Figure 35: User story template.

Here are some examples of user stories from tech.gsa.gov:

- As a Content Owner, I want to be able to create product content so that I can provide information and market to customers.

- As an Editor, I want to review content before it is published so that I can ensure it is optimized with correct grammar and tone.

- As a HR Manager, I need to view a candidate's status so that I can manage their application process throughout the recruiting phases.

- As a Marketing Data Analyst, I need to run the Salesforce and Google analytics reports so that I can build the monthly media campaign plans.

To keep our animal shelter example relatively simple, assume our animal shelter and others that are part of the consortium met and determined these are the most popular user stories:

1. As a potential dog adopter, I want to find a particular breed, color, size, and gender, so that I get the type of dog I am looking for. I want to ensure that the dog's vaccinations are up to date.

2. As a potential bird adopter, I want to find a particular breed and color so that I get the bird I am looking for.

3. As a potential cat adopter, I want to find a particular color and gender, so that I get the type of cat I am looking for.

2. Capture queries

Next, we capture the queries for the one or more user stories within our initiative's scope. While we want to capture multiple user stories to ensure we have a firm grasp of the scope, having just a single user story that drives a NoSQL application is ok. A query starts off with a "verb" and is an action to do something. Some NoSQL database vendors use the phrase "access pattern" instead of query. We will use the term "query" to also encompass "access pattern".

Here are the queries that satisfy our three user stories:

Q1: Only show pets available for adoption.

Q2: Search available dogs by breed, color, size, and gender that have up-to-date vaccinations.

Q3: Search available birds by breed and color.

Q4: Search available cats by color and gender.

Now that we have direction, we can work with the business experts to identify and define the terms within the initiative's scope.

Recall our definition of a term as a noun that represents a collection of business data and is considered both basic and critical to your audience for a particular initiative. A term can fit into one of six categories: who, what, when, where, why, or how. We can use these six categories to create a terms template, a handy brainstorming tool for capturing the terms on our BTM. See Figure 36.

WHO?	WHAT?	WHEN?	WHERE?	WHY?	HOW?

Figure 36: Terms template.

We met again with Mary and came up with this completed template in Figure 37, based on our queries. Notice that this is a brainstorming session, and terms might appear on this template but not on the relational BTM. Excluded terms fit into three categories:

- **Too detailed**. Attributes will appear on the LDM and not the BTM. For example, **Vaccination Date** is more detailed than **Pet** and **Breed**.

- **Out of scope**. Brainstorming is a great way to test the scope of the initiative. Often, terms added to the terms template require additional discussions to determine whether they are in scope. For example, **Surrenderer** and **Adopter** we know are out of scope for the animal shelter's initiative.

- **Redundancies**. Why and How can be very similar. For example, the event **Vaccinate** is documented by the **Vaccination**. The event **Adopt** is documented by **Adoption**. Therefore, we may not need both the event and documentation. In this case, we choose the documentation. That is, we choose How instead of Why.

WHO ?	WHAT ?	WHEN ?	WHERE ?	WHY ?	HOW ?
SURRENDERER	PET	VACCINATION DATE	CRATE	VACCINATE	VACCINATION
ADOPTER	DOG			ADOPT	ADOPTION
	CAT			PROMOTE	PROMOTION
	BIRD				
	BREED				
	GENDER				
	COLOR				
	SIZE				
	IMAGE				

Figure 37: Initially completed template for our animal shelter.

After taking a lunch break, we met again with Mary and refined our terms template, as shown in Figure 38.

WHO ?	WHAT ?	WHEN ?	WHERE ?	WHY ?	HOW ?
~~SURRENDERER~~	PET	~~VACCINATION DATE~~	~~CRATE~~	~~VACCINATE~~	VACCINATION
~~ADOPTER~~	DOG			~~ADOPT~~	~~ADOPTION~~
	CAT			~~PROMOTE~~	~~PROMOTION~~
	BIRD				
	BREED				
	GENDER				
	COLOR				
	SIZE				
	IMAGE				

Figure 38: Refined template for our animal shelter.

We might have a lot of questions during this brainstorming session. It is a great idea to ask questions as they come up. There are three benefits of raising questions:

- **Become known as the detective**. Become comfortable with the level of detective work needed to arrive at a precise set of terms. Look for holes in the definition where ambiguity can sneak in, and ask questions for which the answers will make the definition precise. Consider the question, "Can a pet be of more than one breed?" The answer to this question will refine how the consortium views pets, breeds, and their relationship. A skilled detective remains pragmatic as well, careful to avoid "analysis paralysis". A skilled data modeler must also be pragmatic to ensure the delivery of value to the project team.

- **Uncover hidden terms**. Often the answers to questions lead to more terms on our BTM—terms that we might have missed otherwise. For example, better understanding the relationship between **Vaccination** and **Pet** might lead to more terms on our BTM.

- **Better now than later**. The resulting BTM offers a lot of value, yet the process of getting to that final model is also valuable. Debates and questions challenge people, make them rethink and, in some cases, defend their perspectives. If questions are not raised and answered during the process of building the BTM, the questions will be raised and need to be addressed later in the lifecycle of the initiative, often in the form of data and process surprises, when changes are time-consuming and expensive. Even simple questions like "Are there other attributes that we could use to describe a pet?" can lead to a healthy debate resulting in a more precise BTM.

Here are definitions for each term:

Pet	A dog, cat, or bird that is ready and available to be adopted. An animal becomes a pet after they have passed certain exams administered by our shelter staff.
Gender	The biological sex of the pet. There are three values that we use at the shelter: • Male • Female • Unknown The unknown value is when we are unsure of the gender.
Size	The size is most relevant for dogs, and there are three values that we assign at the shelter: • Small • Medium • Large Cats and birds are assigned medium, except for kittens which are assigned small and parrots which are large.
Color	The primary shade of the pet's fur, feathers, or coat. Examples of colors include brown, red, gold, cream, and black. If a pet has multiple colors, we either assign a primary color or assign a more general term to encompass multiple colors, such as textured, spotted, or patched.
Breed	From Wikipedia, because this definition applies to our initiative: *A breed is a specific group of domestic animals having homogeneous appearance, homogeneous behavior, and/or other characteristics that distinguish it from other organisms of the same species.*
Vaccina -tion	A shot given to a pet to protect it from disease. Examples of vaccinations are rabies for dogs and cats, and polyomavirus vaccine for birds.

Image	A photograph taken of the pet that will be posted on the website.
Dog	From Wikipedia, because this definition applies to our initiative: *The dog is a domesticated descendant of the wolf. Also called the domestic dog, it is derived from the extinct Pleistocene wolf, and the modern wolf is the dog's nearest living relative. Dogs were the first species to be domesticated by hunter-gatherers over 15,000 years ago before the development of agriculture.*
Cat	From Wikipedia, because this definition applies to our initiative: *The cat is a domestic species of small carnivorous mammal. It is the only domesticated species in the family Felidae and is commonly referred to as the domestic cat or house cat to distinguish it from the wild members of the family.*
Bird	From Wikipedia, because this definition applies to our initiative: *Birds are a group of warm-blooded vertebrates constituting the class Aves, characterized by feathers, toothless beaked jaws, the laying of hard-shelled eggs, a high metabolic rate, a four-chambered heart, and a strong yet lightweight skeleton.*

Step 3: Capture the relationships

Even though this is a query BTM, we can ask the Participation and Existence questions to precisely display the business rules for each relationship. Participation questions determine whether there is a "one" or a "many" symbol on the relationship line next to each term. Existence questions determine whether there is a zero (may) or one (must) symbol on the relationship line next to either term. Working with Mary, we identify these relationships on the model:

- **Pet** can be a **Bird, Cat,** or **Dog.** (Subtyping)
- **Pet** and **Image.**
- **Pet** and **Breed.**
- **Pet** and **Gender.**
- **Pet** and **Color.**
- **Pet** and **Vaccination.**
- **Pet** and **Size.**

Table 5 contains the answers to the Participation and Existence questions for each of these seven relationships (excluding the subtyping relationship, so six actually). After translating the answer to each question into the model, we have the animal shelter BTM in Figure 39.

Question	Yes	No
Can a Gender categorize more than one Pet?	✓	
Can a Pet be categorized by more than one Gender?		✓
Can a Gender exist without a Pet?	✓	
Can a Pet exist without a Gender?		✓
Can a Size categorize more than one Pet?	✓	
Can a Pet be categorized by more than one Size?		✓
Can a Size exist without a Pet?	✓	
Can a Pet exist without a Size?		✓
Can a Color describe more than one Pet?	✓	
Can a Pet be described by more than one Color?		✓
Can a Color exist without a Pet?	✓	
Can a Pet exist without a Color?		✓

Question	Yes	No
Can a Pet be described by more than one Breed?	✓	
Can a Breed describe more than one Pet?	✓	
Can a Pet exist without a Breed?		✓
Can a Breed exist without a Pet?	✓	
Can a Pet be given more than one Vaccination?	✓	
Can a Vaccination be given to more than one Pet?	✓	
Can a Pet exist without a Vaccination?	✓	
Can a Vaccination exist without a Pet?	✓	
Can a Pet take more than one Image?	✓	
Can an Image be taken of more than one Pet?	✓	
Can a Pet exist without an Image?		✓
Can an Image exist without a Pet?		✓

Table 5: Answers to the Participation and Existence questions.

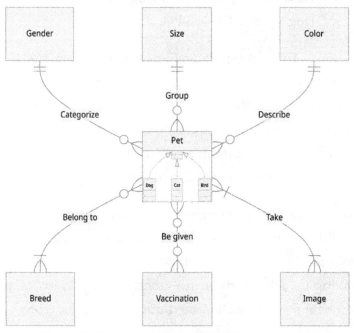

Figure 39: Our animal shelter BTM (showing rules).

These relationships are read as:

- Each **Gender** may categorize many **Pets**.
- Each **Pet** must be categorized by one **Gender**.
- Each **Size** may group many **Pets**.
- Each **Pet** must be grouped by one **Size**.
- Each **Color** may describe many **Pets**.
- Each **Pet** must be described by one **Color**.
- Each **Pet** must belong to many **Breeds**.
- Each **Breed** may be assigned to many **Pets**.
- Each **Pet** may be given many **Vaccinations**.
- Each **Vaccination** may be given to many **Pets**.
- Each **Pet** must take many **Images**.
- Each **Image** must be taken of many **Pets**.
- Each **Pet** may either be a **Dog**, **Cat**, or **Bird**.
- **Dog** is a **Pet**. **Cat** is a **Pet**. **Bird** is a **Pet**.

The answers to the participation and existence questions are context-dependent. That is, the scope of the initiative determines the answers. In this case, because our scope is the subset of the animal shelter's business that will be used as part of this consortium's project, we know at this point that a **Pet** must be described by only one **Color**.

Even though we determined that a TerminusDB database should be used to answer these queries, you can see how the traditional data model provides value in terms of making us ask the right questions and then providing a powerful communication medium showing the terms and their business rules. Even if we are not implementing our solution in a relational database, this BTM provides value.

Build a relational data model even though the solution is in a NoSQL database such as TerminusDB, if you feel there can be value. That is, if you feel there is value in explaining the terms with precision along with their business rules, build the relational BTM. If you feel there is value in organizing the attributes into sets using normalization, build the relational LDM. It will help you organize your thoughts and provide you with a very effective communication tool.

Our end goal, though, is to create a TerminusDB database. Therefore, we need a query BTM. So, we need to determine the order in which someone would run the queries.

Graphing the sequence of queries leads to the query BTM. The query BTM is a numbered list of all queries necessary to deliver the user stories within the initiative's scope. The model also shows a sequence or dependency among the queries. The query BTM for our four queries would look like what appears in Figure 40.

All the queries depend on the first query. That is, we first need to filter by pets available for adoption.

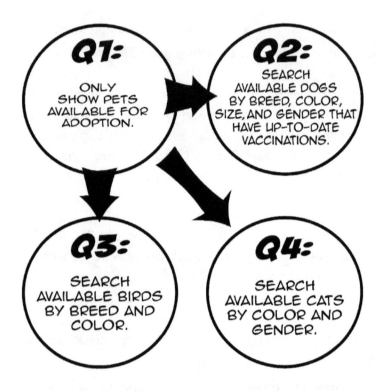

Figure 40: Our animal shelter BTM (showing queries).

Step 4: Determine the visual

Someone will need to review your work and use your model as input for future deliverables such as software development, so deciding on the most useful visual is an important step. After getting an answer to Strategic Question #4, *Who is our audience?*, we know that Mary will be our validator.

There are many ways of displaying the BTM. Factors include the technical competence of the audience and the existing tools environment.

However, it would be helpful to know which data modeling notations and data modeling tools are currently being used within the organization. If the audience is familiar with a particular data modeling notation—such as Information Engineering (IE), which we have been using throughout this book—that is the notation we should use. If the audience is familiar with a particular data modeling tool, and that data modeling tool uses a different notation, we should use that tool with that notation to create the BTM.

Luckily, the two BTMs we created, one for rules and one for queries, are very intuitive, so there is a very good chance our models will be well-understood by the audience.

Step 5: Review and confirm

Previously we identified the person or group responsible for validating the model. Now we need to show them the model and make sure it is correct. Often at this stage, after reviewing the model, we make some changes and then show them the model again. This iterative cycle continues until the validator approves the model.

Three tips

1. **Organization.** The steps you went through in building this "model" are the same steps we go through in building any model. It is all about organizing information. Data modelers are fantastic organizers. We take the chaotic real world and show it in a precise form, creating powerful communication tools.

2. **80/20 Rule.** Don't go for perfection. Too many requirements meetings end with unfulfilled goals by spending too much time discussing a minute particular issue. After a few minutes of discussion, if you feel the issue's discussion may take up too much time and not lead to a resolution, document the issue and keep going. You will find that for modeling to work well with Agile and other iterative approaches, you may have to forego perfection and sometimes even completion. Much better to document the unanswered questions and issues and keep going. Much better to deliver something imperfect yet still very valuable than deliver nothing. You will find that you can get the data model about 80% complete in 20% of the time. One of your deliverables will be a document containing unanswered questions and unresolved issues. Once all these issues and questions are resolved, which will take about 80% of your time to complete, the model will be 100% complete.

3. **Diplomacy.** As William Kent said in **Data and Reality** (1978), *so, once again, if we are going to have a database about books, before we can know what one representative stands for, we had better have a consensus among all users as to what "one book" is.* Invest time trying to get consensus on terms before building a solution. Imagine someone querying on pets without having a clear definition of what a pet is.

Three takeaways

1. Six strategic questions must be asked before you begin any project (Step 1). These questions are a prerequisite to the success of any initiative because they ensure we choose the right terms for our BTM. Next, identify all terms within the scope of the initiative (Step 2). Make sure each term is clearly and completely defined. Then determine how these terms are related (Step 3). Often, you will need to go back to Step 2 at this point, because in capturing relationships, you may come up with new terms. Next, determine the most beneficial visual for your audience (Step 4). Consider the visual that would resonate best with those needing to review and use your BTM. As a final step, seek approval of your BTM (Step 5). Often at this point, there are additional changes to the model, and we cycle through these steps until the model is accepted.

2. Create a relational BTM in addition to a query BTM if you feel there would be value in capturing and explaining the participation and existence rules.

3. Never underestimate the value of precise and complete definitions.

Refine

This chapter will explain the data modeling refine phase. We explain the purpose of refine, refine the model for our animal shelter case study, and then walk through the refine approach. We end the chapter with three tips and three takeaways.

Purpose

The purpose of the refinement stage is to create the logical data model (LDM) based on our common business vocabulary defined during the align stage. Refine is how the modeler captures the business requirements without complicating the model with implementation concerns, such as software and hardware. The shelter's Logical Data Model (LDM) uses the common business language from the BTM to precisely define the business requirements. The LDM is fully attributed yet independent of technology. We build the relational LDM by normalizing, covered in Chapter 1. Figure 41 contains the shelter's relational LDM.

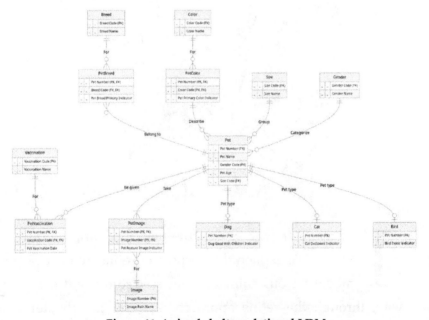

Figure 41: Animal shelter relational LDM.

This model does not change based on requirements. Therefore, we can use it as the starting point model for all queries. Let's briefly walk through the model. The shelter identifies each **Pet** with a **Pet Number**, which is a unique counter assigned to the **Pet** the day the **Pet** arrives. Also entered at this time are the pet's name (**Pet Name**) and age (**Pet Age**). If the **Pet** does not have a name, it is given one by the shelter employee entering the pet's information. If the age is unknown, it is estimated by the shelter employee entering the pet's information. If the **Pet** is a **Dog**, the shelter employee entering the information performs a few assessments to determine whether the Dog is good with children (**Dog Good With Children Indicator**). If the **Pet** is a **Cat**, the shelter employee determines whether the **Cat** has been declawed (**Cat Declawed Indicator**). If the Pet is a **Bird**, the shelter employee enters whether it is an exotic bird such as a parrot (**Bird Exotic Indicator**).

Approach

The refine stage is all about determining the business requirements for the initiative. The end goal is a logical data model which captures the attributes and relationships needed to answer the queries. The steps to complete appear in Figure 42.

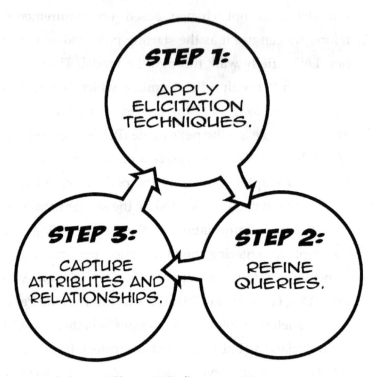

Figure 42: Refinement steps.

Similar to determining the more detailed structures in a traditional logical data model, we determine the more detailed structures needed to deliver the queries during the refinement stage. You can therefore call the query LDM a query refinement model if you prefer. The query refinement model is all about discovery and captures the answers to the queries that reveal insights into a business process.

Step 1: Apply elicitation techniques

This is where we interact with the business stakeholders to identify the attributes and relationships needed to answer the queries. We keep refining, usually until we run out of time. Techniques we can use include interviewing, artifact analysis (studying existing or proposed business or technical documents), job shadowing (watching someone work), and prototyping. You can use any combination of these techniques to obtain the attributes and relationships to answer the queries. Often these techniques are used within an Agile framework. You choose which techniques to use based on your starting point and the needs of the stakeholders. For example, if a stakeholder says, "I don't know what I want, but I'll know when I see it," building a prototype might be the best approach.

Analyze workloads

An important part of this exercise is to identify, quantify, and qualify the workload.

You need to identify each operation as either a read or a write operation, and you need to understand the read-to-write ratio. Make a list of all Create, Read, Update, and Delete (CRUD) operations, and take the time to go through the exercise of drawing wireframes of screens and reports, and of assembling workflow diagrams. Thinking these through and validating them with subject matter experts will inevitably reveal facts you might have previously overlooked.

For write operations, you want to know for how long to hold data (retention), the frequency by which data is transmitted to the system, average document size, and expectation of durability (how often data is written from memory to disk, with what level of acknowledgement, to what degree of replication, etc.). Start your design exercise with the most critical operation and work your way down the list.

For read operations, you also want to document the patterns and required freshness of the data, taking into account eventual consistency and read latency. Data freshness is related to replication time if you read from a secondary, or to the acceptable time for a piece of data derived (computed, for example) from other pieces. It defines how fast written data must be accessible for read operations: immediately (data consistent at all times), within 10 milliseconds, 1 second, 1 minute, 1 hour, 1 day, etc. For example, reading the top reviews associated with a product, which are cached in a product document, may have a tolerated 1-day freshness. Read latency is typically specified in milliseconds, where p95 and p99 values represent the 95th and 99th percentile values, respectively (a read latency p95 value of 100ms means that 95 out of 100 requests took 100ms or less to complete.) You should also document query predicates, that is, the specific expressions and parameters used to determine which documents should be retrieved for a query.

This information helps validate the choice of physical design of documents and attributes, may orient necessary indexes, and impacts the sizing and provisioning of the hardware, hence the budget for the project. Different data modeling patterns result in different impacts on read performance, number of write operations, cost of indexes, etc. So, you may have to make compromises and balance needs that are sometimes contradictory.

You may use a spreadsheet or any other method to document the results of your workload analysis. When considering schema evolution later in the lifecycle, you will be able to review the values originally recorded, as reality might be very different than what was originally estimated.

There are a few broad categories of search that may inform physical-model needs of queries, so you may wish to document queries as being one of these types of search:

- **Standard**: marks queries based on one or more fields in a document.

- **Geospatial**: allows for efficient retrieval of documents based on their geographic location or proximity to a specific point.

- **Text**: search for text within fields when efficient and relevance-based searches across large volumes of text-based data are required.

Quantify relationships

Since the advent of entity relationship diagrams, we restricted ourselves to using zero, one, and many as the different cardinalities of relationships.

This may have been appropriate for the longest time; however, the world has changed. Datasets are a few orders of magnitude larger than they were a few years ago. Not understanding that a relationship's "many" side may refer to thousands or millions of objects and trying to embed, pull, or join these objects may not work well for most applications. Because these humongous relationships are more frequent than before, we suggest quantifying them not just with "many" but with actual numbers. For example, instead of using [0, M] to say that an object can be linked to zero-to-many objects, we should try to quantify these numbers whenever possible. For example, a product may have [0, 1000] reviews. This is more telling. For example, writing 1000 down makes us think about pagination and possibly limiting the number of reviews on a product when it reaches the maximum value.

To increase our knowledge about the relationship, we can add an optional "most likely" or "median" value. For example, [0, 20, 1000] is more descriptive by telling us that a product may have 0 to 1000 reviews with a median of 20.

Yes, we will get these numbers wrong, especially at the beginning. However, we should aim to get the order of magnitude right. If we don't get that right, it is a red flag to review the model. Maybe a piece of information should not be embedded (for example, as a subdocument in TerminusDB) but referenced instead.

Step 2: Refine queries

The refinement process is iterative, and we keep refining, again, usually until we run out of time.

Step 3: Capture attributes and relationships

Ideally, because of the hierarchical nature of document (and also key-value) databases, we should strive to answer one or more queries with a single logical structure. Although this might seem "anti-normalization", one structure organized to a particular query can be faster and simpler than connecting multiple structures. The logical data model contains the attributes and related structures needed for each of the queries identified in the query refinement model.

Using artifact analysis, we can start with the animal shelter's logical model and use this model as a good way to capture the attributes and relationships within our scope. Based on the queries, quite a few of our concepts are not directly needed for search or filtering, and so they can become additional descriptive attributes on the **Pet** entity.

For example, no critical queries involved vaccinations. Therefore, we can simplify this model subset from the model in Figure 43 to the model in Figure 44.

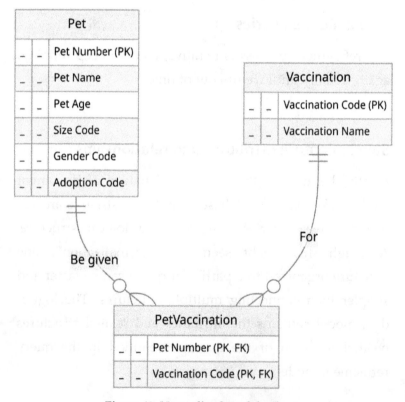

Figure 43: Normalized model subset.

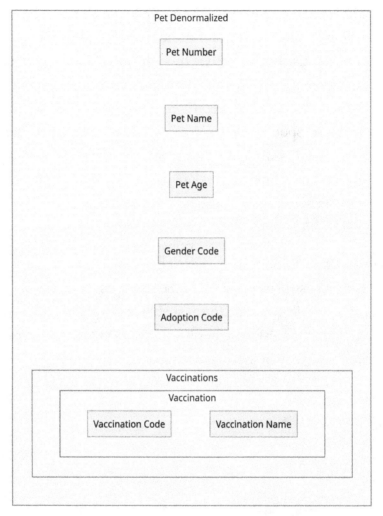

Figure 44: Denormalized model subset.

This example illustrates how traditional RDBMS models differ from NoSQL. On our original relational-perspective logical model, it was important to communication that a **Pet** can receive many **Vaccinations** and a **Vaccination** can be given to many **Pets**. In our NoSQL query-perspective logical model, however, since there were no queries needing to filter or search by vaccination, the vaccination attributes just become other descriptive attributes of **Pet**. The **Vaccination Code** and **Vaccination Name** attributes are now attributes of records nested within **Pet**. So, for example, if Spot the Dog had five vaccinations, they would all be listed within Spot's record (or *document* to use TerminusDB terminology). Following this same logic, the pet's colors and images also become nested sets, as shown in Figure 45.

In addition, to help with querying, we may wish to create a **Pet Type** structure instead of the subtypes, **Dog**, **Cat**, and **Bird**. After determining the available pets for adoption, we wish to distinguish whether the **Pet** is a **Dog**, **Cat**, or **Bird**. Our model may look like what appears in Figure 46.

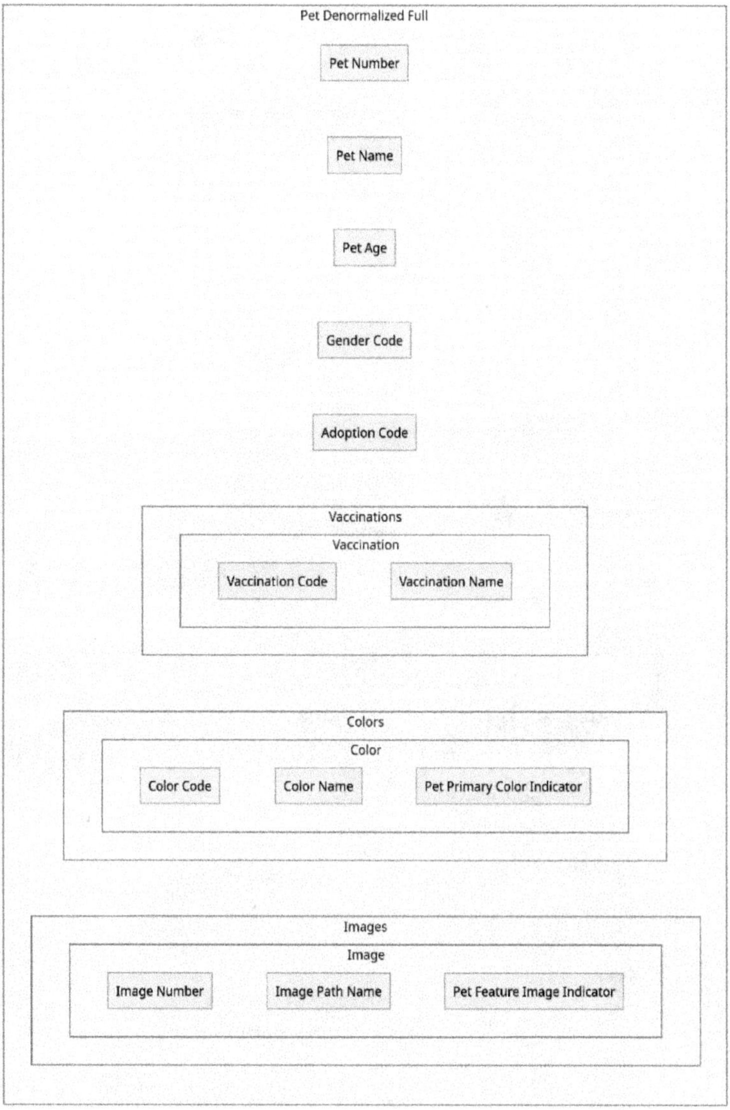

Figure 45: Nested arrays added for color and images.

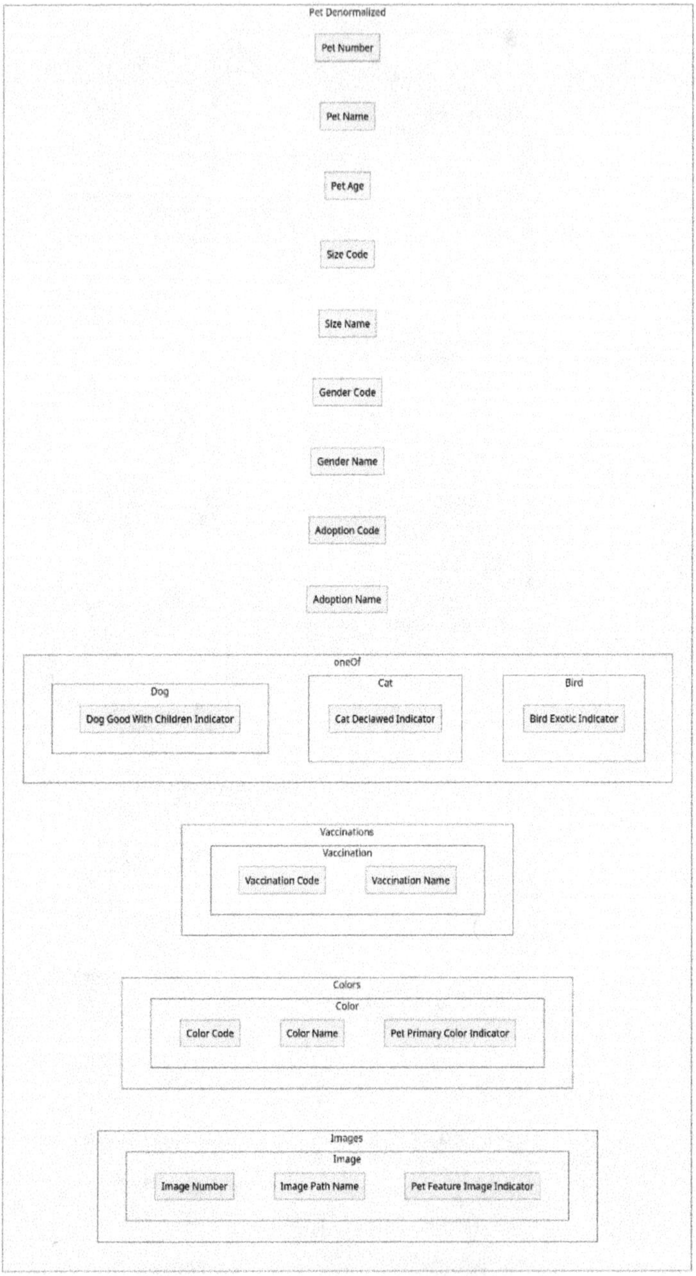

Figure 46: A complete LDM with Pet Type.

This example illustrates the polymorphic nature of a document model as an alternative to something like class inheritance. This single-document schema describes and can validate different document types for dogs, cats, and birds, in addition to the common structure. Relational subtyping is accomplished here with a oneOf attribute that expresses mutually exclusive and collectively exhaustive subschemas. Junction tables found in relational models are replaced here by sets of sub-objects, or arrays if ordering of items is significant.

However, with TerminusDB, we can leverage class inheritance for document definitions, so we can retain the visual clarity of the notion of inheritance in our logical model, as shown in Figure 47. We have also decided to model pet size and pet gender as enumerations in the logical model, that is, as a set of symbolic names (members) that represent unique and constant values, as informed by our align-stage term definitions. Finally, even though we may designate image, vaccination, etc. information as subdocuments within a Pet-typed document in a physical model, we choose to retain that information as logically distinct in our final LDM diagram.

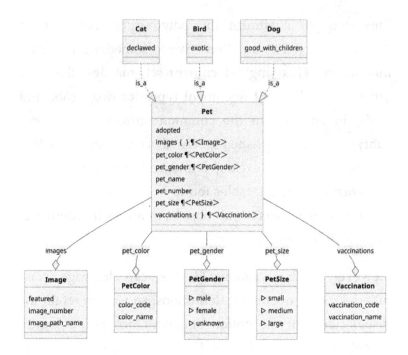

Figure 47: A complete LDM with inheritance and enumeration types.

Three tips

1. **Access patterns:** the query-driven approach is critical to leverage the benefits of NoSQL when creating an LDM. Don't be tempted by old normalization habits unless the workload analysis reveals relationship cardinality that warrants normalization.

2. **Aggregates:** keep together what belongs together. A nested logical structure in a single document (a subdocument or array/list/set of subdocuments) can

ensure atomicity and consistency of inserts, updates, and queries without custom joins. It is also beneficial for developers who are used to working with objects, and it is easier to understand for humans.

3. **It is easier to normalize a denormalized structure than the opposite:** a normalized LDM is technology-agnostic neither if it includes supertypes/subtypes or junction tables, nor if your physical targets are exclusively relational and don't include NoSQL. A denormalized LDM on the other hand, can be easily normalized for relational physical targets by a good data modeling tool, while providing denormalized structures based on the access patterns identified earlier. Thus, an LDM in the style of Figure 46 may be preferable to one in the style of Figure 47.

Three takeaways

1. The purpose of the refinement stage is to create the logical data model (LDM) based on our common business vocabulary, defined for our initiative during the align stage. Refine is how the modeler captures the business requirements without complicating the model with implementation concerns, such as software and hardware.

2. An LDM is typically fully attributed yet independent of technology. But this strict definition is being challenged nowadays with the fact that technology targets can be so different in nature: relational databases, the different families of NoSQL, storage formats for data lakes, pub/sub pipelines, APIs, etc.

3. It used to be, with relational databases, that you wanted to design a structure that could handle any possible future query that might be run down the road. With NoSQL, you may want to design schemas that are specific, not only for an application, but for each access pattern (write or read) in that application.

CHAPTER 3

Design

This chapter will explain the data modeling design phase. We explain the purpose of design, design the model for our animal shelter case study, and then walk through the design approach. We end the chapter with three tips and three takeaways.

Purpose

The purpose of the design stage is to create the physical data model (PDM) based on the business requirements defined on our logical data model. Design is how the modeler captures the technical requirements without compromising the business requirements and also accommodating the initiative's software and technology needs used for the initiative.

The design stage is also where we accommodate history. That is, we modify our structures to capture how data changes over time. For example, the Design stage would allow us to keep track of not just the most recent name for a pet, but also the original. For example, the animal shelter may change a pet's name from Sparky to Daisy. Our design could store the original pet name and the most current, so we would know Daisy's original name was Sparky. Although this is not a book on temporal data or modeling approaches that gracefully allow for storage subject to high data volatility or varying history requirements, such as the Data Vault,[3] you would need to consider such factors in the Design stage.

Figure 48 shows the Physical Data Model (PDM) of the animal shelter's Microsoft Access database design.

----

[3] For more on the data vault, read John Giles' *The Elephant in the Fridge*.

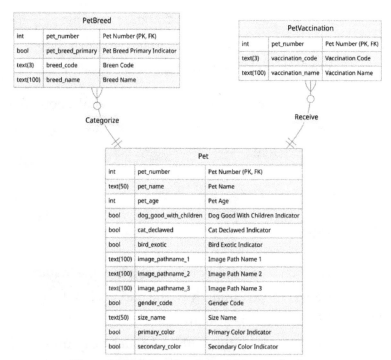

Figure 48: PDM of the shelter's Access database

Note that the PDM includes formatting and nullability. Also, this model is heavily denormalized. For example:

- Although the logical model communicates that a **Pet** can have any number of images, their design only allows up to three images for each **Pet**. The shelter uses **Image_Path_Name_1** for the featured image.

- Notice how some coded entities from the logical model have been addressed. **Gender_Name** is not needed because everyone knows the codes. People are not familiar with **Size_Code,** so only

Size_Name is stored. It is common for coded
entities to be modeled in different ways in the
physical model, depending on the requirements.

We're not going to dive into any more detail about the
shelter's existing PDM as presented. Let's design one for
the current initiative.

Approach

The design stage is all about developing the database-
specific design for the initiative. The end goal is the query
PDM, which we can also call the *query design model*. For our
animal shelter initiative, this model captures the
TerminusDB design and JSON interchange format for the
initiative. The steps to complete appear in Figure 49.

Step 1: Select database(s)

We now know enough to decide which database would be
ideal for the application. Sometimes we might choose more
than one database if we feel it would be the best
architecture for the application. We know in the
consortium's case that they are using JSON for transport
and TerminusDB for storage.

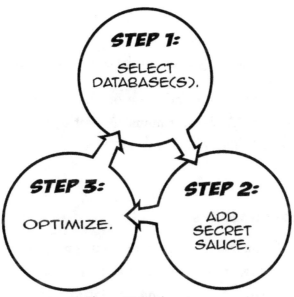

Figure 49: Design steps

Why TerminusDB? The consortium was attracted to having:

- both document-oriented and graph-oriented query and retrieval capabilities, to allow for fine-grained search but also simple document-grain retrieval for display;

- ACID transactions, to ease concern about consortium members having differing interpretations of the desired schema;

- revision control and access to full database update history through git-like commits, to ease undoing data entry mistakes and to track the provenance of information entered; and

- RDF triples as the underlying format for consortium member data contributions, to ease data integration for the consortium website.

We won't dive deep into these or other reasons why an initiative may choose TerminusDB. Rather, we'll focus on creating a PDM to support the initiative.

Step 2: Add secret sauce

Although many document-oriented or graph-oriented NoSQL databases can be quite similar in some respects, each database has something special to consider during design. For example, for TerminusDB, we would consider where to use their secret sauce, such as TerminusDB-specific functionality like the following:

- (Multiple) inheritance of classes
- Mutually exclusive (sets of) properties
- Subdocuments, as well as "Unfoldable" top-level documents
- Enumeration types
- Various primary-key auto-generation mechanisms
- Abstract classes
- Type families, including Sets and Sets with min/max/exact cardinalities, not just ordered Lists or Arrays

We will walk through and demonstrate much of the above functionality via our PDM, shown in Figure 50. We will explore each element of this and explain how it maps our logical model to a physical model for TerminusDB.

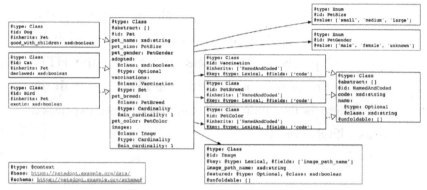

Figure 50: Our TerminusDB PDM.

The first thing you may notice about the PDM diagram in Figure 50 is the strange notation in each box. Here's the content from one of the boxes, as a JSON object:

```
// The Context
{
  "@type": "@context",
  "@base": "https://petadopt.example.org/data/",
  "@schema": "https://petadopt.example.org/schema#"
}
```

This JSON object is a valid element of a TerminusDB schema, which is expressed as a JSON list of objects. So, the PDM is in a form that can be directly translated to what is effectively the Data Definition Language of TerminusDB. TerminusDB takes a cue from the JSON-LD standard and designates JSON key names starting with

"@" as special "keyword" keys that are distinct from user-supplied property keys (which don't start with "@"). Each TerminusDB schema has a distinct object with the {"@type": "@context"} key-value pair. That is, a singleton "@context"-typed object, that provides URI prefixes for all data elements (via @base) and schema elements (via @schema). This enables all resources to have globally unique and persistent identifiers under, e.g., the HTTP DNS authority of the consortium. The PDM box with the most content is the main "Pet" (abstract) class, expressed here as a JSON object:

```
// The Pet (abstract) Class
{
  "@type": "Class",
  "@abstract": [],
  "@id": "Pet",
  "pet_name": "xsd:string",
  "pet_size": "PetSize",
  "pet_gender": "PetGender",
  "adopted": {
    "@class": "xsd:boolean",
    "@type": "Optional"
  },
  "vaccinations": {
    "@class": "Vaccination",
    "@type": "Set"
  },
  "pet_breed": {
    "@class": "PetBreed",
    "@type": "Cardinality",
    "@min_cardinality": 1
  },
  "pet_color": "PetColor",
  "images": {
    "@class": "Image",
    "@type": "Cardinality",
    "@min_cardinality": 1
  }
}
```

TerminusDB uses some terminology common to object-oriented programming in the document-oriented perspective it supports (it also supports a graph-oriented perspective, as we will see later). Instead of sets of entities being called *tables* as in RDBMs, *collections* in MongoDB, etc., they are *classes* in TerminusDB.

Notice that there is no "pet number" in the PDM. The role of this attribute in the LDM was as a unique identifier for a Pet – there is no significance given to the actual numeric value. Since TerminusDB is also a graph database, each entity is a graph node with a unique identifier. In the JSON-LD document-oriented representation of RDF graph nodes, we use the special "@id" key to convey a node's identifier, and TerminusDB uses this as well. A class definition may have a "@key" key-value pair as a directive for generating the unique suffix of a class instance's identifier. This directive defaults to {"@key": {"@type": "Random"}}. That is, generate a random string. In TerminusDB, a document identifier is a concatenation of (a) the context's @base URI, (b) a URI path identifying the class of entity ("Pet/" in this case), and (c) the key generated by the @key spec. There are other @key options that are functions of the supplied content of a class instance; we will see an example of another one shortly.

The *pet_name* property is given a range of "xsd:string". "xsd:" is a prefix that represents the URI namespace for the W3C XML Schema Definition Language (XSD) Datatypes, which is <https://www.w3.org/2001/XMLSchema#>. This means that "xsd:string" is short for <https://www.w3.org/2001/XMLSchema#string> (more human-friendly documentation is at <https://www.w3.org/TR/xmlschema-2/#string>, though). TerminusDB supports many of the W3C XSD types as class property ranges, like xsd:positiveInteger for integer numbers greater than 0.

The *pet_size* property has a range of PetSize, which in turn is defined in the PDM as:

```
// The PetSize Enumeration
{
  "@type": "Enum",
  "@id": "PetSize",
  "@value": ["small", "medium", "large"]
}
```

Based on the term definition of Pet Size we gathered in our BTM, we defined PetSize as a fixed Enumeration pseudo-class rather than as a normal TerminusDB class. The *pet_gender* property, with a range of PetGender, has a similarly defined Enumeration based on our BTM term definition.

For the *adopted* property, we use a range class of xsd:boolean, but we also use the "Optional" type-family marker to qualify the property range as optional. We did this to allow more-forgiving data entry: when *adopted* is missing from a Pet instance, we will assume that means "not adopted" (equivalent to an explicit {"adopted": "false"}). In other initiatives, we may instead wish to interpret the absence of a property value as "I don't know," but for this initiative we assume that a pet's adoption status is always true or false. Note that, unlike a traditional RDBMS, records are not fixed-size tuples, so we don't need to store explicit values for every known properly. That is, we don't need to store a default value or a special "null" value.

The *vaccinations* property is specified as a Set (an unordered collection) of Vaccination instances. We will go over the definition of the Vaccination class later. For now, what is important to note about this facility of TerminusDB is that (a) it allows one to be explicit about the unordered-ness of a Pet's vaccinations, whereas many other database systems overload a list/array type for both ordered and unordered collections; and (b) due to the underlying RDF data representation used by TerminusDB, there is no concern about unrestrained growth of a Set-typed property range for a given document, as set elements are not physical stored "in a" document. Rather, a "document" in TerminusDB is a logical construct that simplifies both transactional integrity and retrieval for "all of" a thing (a Pet in this case). As such, there is no performance tradeoff as in some other database systems to linking from a Pet to its vaccinations versus from a Vaccination to its pet, which is not a relevant decision for this initiative because the number of vaccinations per pet will not number in the thousands or more, but which may be relevant for other initiatives. With RDF subject-predicate-object triples, it is as simple to retrieve a subject's objects for a given predicate as it is to retrieve an object's subjects for that same predicate, and this holds for TerminusDB given its underlying RDF representation.

The *pet_breed* property has a type-family-qualified range class just like *adopted* and *vaccinations*, but the type family is Cardinality. What does this mean? You can think of Cardinality as a subtype of Set, with the additional benefit of being able to annotate a Cardinality-qualified property range with minimum, maximum, or exact (i.e., equal minimum and maximum) cardinalities. We define *pet_breed* as a Set of PetBreed elements containing at least one element at all times, that is, as a Cardinality with a @min_cardinality of 1.

From our BTM term definitions, we noted that, although a pet may have more than one color, a single color is assigned to a pet – either a primary color, or a term that represents a mix of some kind. Thus, our range class for *pet_color* is simply PetColor, rather than being qualified as optional or as a collection of some kind.

The final class property of Pet is *images*, with a range class of Image qualified as being a cardinality-constrained set (Cardinality) with a minimum cardinality of 1.

We have walked through the property elements of our Pet class. Let's now jog leftward in the PDM diagram of Figure 50, to our subtypes of Pet, or in the nomenclature of TerminusDB schema definition, the classes that inherit from Pet. Here is a JSON representation of Dog, directly insertable into TerminusDB via, for example, the `doc insert DB_SPEC --graph-type schema` command-line interface (CLI) subcommand:

```
{
  "@type": "Class",
  "@id": "Dog",
  "@inherits": "Pet",
  "good_with_children": "xsd:boolean"
}
```

The @inherits key tells us that a Dog inherits all the property-key specifications from Pet. Note that unlike what you may be familiar with in many object-oriented programming languages, inheritance here is restricted to data properties. There is no sense in which methods/behavior is inherited, as any functionality attributed to a TerminusDB class in a given application would be defined entirely at the application layer, not at the data layer. Our "good with children" indicator has as its range class the standard XML Schema Definition's Boolean datatype (https://www.w3.org/TR/xmlschema-2/#boolean).

Here's an example Dog document to insert:

```
{
  "@type": "Dog",
  "pet_name": "Sparky",
  "pet_size": "small",
  "pet_gender": "male",
  "pet_breed": {
    "code": "mutt"
  },
  "pet_color": {
    "code": "spotted"
  },
  "images": {
    "image_path_name": "sparky.jpg"
  },
  "good_with_children": true
}
```

The resulting document in the database will have an @id such as `<https://petadopt.example.org/data/Dog/4C4ZLvRVDDHV0xJA>`. Note that since the Dog class does not supply a @key spec, the suffix of a Dog's @id is a randomly generated string.

The definitions of Cat and Bird are like that of Dog, but substituting their respective indicators of interest:

```
{
  "@type": "Class",
  "@id": "Cat",
  "@inherits": "Pet",
  "declawed": "xsd:boolean"
}
{
  "@type": "Class",
  "@id": "Bird",
  "@inherits": "Pet",
  "exotic": "xsd:boolean"
}
```

Moving to the right of the Pet-definition node in Figure 50, we see these definitions of *Vaccination*, *PetBreed*, and *PetColor*:

```
{
  "@type": "Class",
  "@id": "Vaccination",
  "@inherits": ["NamedAndCoded"],
  "@key": {"@type": "Lexical", "@fields": ["code"]}
}
{
  "@type": "Class",
  "@id": "PetBreed",
  "@inherits": ["NamedAndCoded"],
  "@key": {"@type": "Lexical", "@fields": ["code"]}
}
{
  "@type": "Class",
  "@id": "PetColor",
  "@inherits": ["NamedAndCoded"],
  "@key": {"@type": "Lexical", "@fields": ["code"]}
}
```

Each of these are "named and coded" classes keyed lexically on their code. What do we mean by this?

```
{
  "@type": "Class",
  "@abstract": [],
  "@id": "NamedAndCoded",
  "code": "xsd:string",
  "name": {
    "@type": "Optional",
    "@class": "xsd:string"
  },
  "@unfoldable": []
}
```

We can see that a *NamedAndCoded* document has been defined as one with a string-valued *code* and, optionally, a string-valued *name*. By inheriting from NamedAndCoded via @inherits, another TerminusDB class can "mix in" these properties (similar to "mix-in" classes in object-oriented programming languages). One can mix in multiple classes (multiple inheritance), which is why the range of @inherits is formatted as a JSON array. Furthermore, a NamedAndCoded document is *unfoldable*, meaning it will be returned as a nested subdocument ("unfolded") as part of the retrieval of any document that references it (by @id). The range class for the @unfoldable key is the so-called "Unit" type, which has a single extension, "[]", and is used when only the presence of a key is interesting, but that key has no interesting value. Notice that the @abstract key is similar in this respect. There is a key related to @unfoldable, namely @subdocument, that is used when an "unfoldable" class is not "top-level", that is, when it "belongs" to its referencing "parent" document. In our initiative, all our NamedAndCoded classes (Vaccination, PetBreed, and PetColor) denote instances that are independent of any Pet from which they are referenced.

Now, what does it mean for a class to be keyed lexically on a sequence of fields, as in {"@key": {"@type": "Lexical", "@fields": ["code"]}}? It means that the suffix of a document's unique ID is recognizable as a simple copying of the given fields' values, modulo URL encoding. For example, if we were to insert a simple Vaccination in the database:

```
echo '{"@type": "Vaccination", "code": "rabies"}' \
  | terminusdb doc insert admin/pet_adoption
```

the resulting document has an @id of:

https://petadopt.example.org/data/Vaccination/rabies

We are now prepared to fully interpret the definitions of *Vaccination, PetBreed,* and *PetColor.* They each have a string-valued *code,* an optional string-valued *name,* any given document's unique ID is reproducible given the same code value as input for a given class, and they each will be "unfolded" and returned, as nested subdocuments alongside a Pet's "top-level" properties, whenever fetching a Pet document from the database.

Our final PDM element is the *Image* class:

```
{
  "@type": "Class",
  "@id": "Image",
  "@key": {
    "@type": "Lexical",
    "@fields": [
      "image_path_name"
    ]
  },
  "image_path_name": "xsd:string",
  "featured": {
    "@type": "Optional",
    "@class": "xsd:boolean"
  },
  "@unfoldable": []
}
```

Now that we know how to interpret the "Lexical"-type @key spec and the @unfoldable key, we can see that an *Image* is uniquely identified by its required string-ranged *image_path_name* value, which is used as the suffix of its @id, that an Image optionally may be flagged as featured (or explicitly flagged as not featured), and that when, for example, a Pet with an Image-ranged property is retrieved, that property's Image reference will be unfolded. That is, the corresponding Image document will be retrieved and transcluded as a subdocument of the retrieved Pet document.

Putting it all together, if we insert this JSON document into our database:

```
{
  "@type": "Dog",
  "pet_name": "Sparky",
  "pet_size": "small",
  "pet_gender": "male",
  "pet_breed": {"code": "mutt"},
  "pet_color": {"code": "spotted"},
  "vaccinations": [{"code": "rabies"}],
  "images": [{"image_path_name": "sparky.jpg"}],
  "good_with_children": true
}
```

then the result of fetching Sparky (har har), e.g.

```
terminusdb    doc    get    admin/pet_adoption    \
--type Dog -q '{"pet_name": "Sparky"}'
```

would look like

```
{
  "@id": "Dog/VIipJUML6Z7HVNWB",
  "@type": "Dog",
  "images": {
    "@id": "Image/sparky.jpg",
    "@type": "Image",
    "image_path_name": "sparky.jpg"
  },
  "pet_breed": {
    "@id": "PetBreed/mutt",
    "@type": "PetBreed",
    "code": "mutt"
  },
  "pet_color": {
    "@id": "PetColor/spotted",
```

```
    "@type": "PetColor",
    "code": "spotted"
  },
  "pet_gender": "male",
  "pet_name": "Sparky",
  "pet_size": "small",
  "vaccinations": [
    {
      "@id": "Vaccination/rabies",
      "@type": "Vaccination",
      "code": "rabies"
    }
  ],
  "good_with_children": true
}
```

For brevity, TerminusDB prepends neither the @base prefix for document @id values nor the @schema prefix for schema elements (property and class names) from a database's @context to the documents returned from queries.

Step 3: Optimize

Similar to indexing, denormalizing, partitioning, and adding views to a RDBMS physical model, we can add additional database-specific features to the query refinement model to produce the query design model.

What follows are some optimization features of TerminusDB, introduced as they may relate to our pet adoption initiative.

Support for both document- and graph-oriented queries

The underlying universal-relation basis ("one table" of triples) of TerminusDB allows comprehensive covering indexes along permutations of (subject, predicate, object), e.g. ("<pet_id>, <pet_name>, "Sparky"). This means that, even though document retrievals are not "zero-hop", meaning a document's key-value pairs are physically co-located in a record keyed on the document id as in table-oriented RDMSes or a document-oriented database such as MongoDB, the set of "one-hop" queries entailed by a document-retrieval request (a request for the graph fragment defined by a class definition as the "neighborhood" of a graph node) is fast, and can be subject to normal strategies for response caching independent of the database service. Furthermore, multi-hop queries that crawl more of a graph, including so-called "path queries" that use regular expressions to describe multi-hop searches concisely, are likewise efficient in TerminusDB. For example, recent benchmarking has determined that TerminusDB is over 50% faster than Neo4j for both single-hop and (multi-hop) path queries.[4]

---

[4] https://terminusdb.com/blog/graph-database-performance-benchmark/ (2023-08-11).

This is to say that, for TerminusDB, decisions about document orientation versus graph orientation are typically matters of modeling for developer and user experience rather than matters of query performance optimization. In other words, there is typically no need for the PDM to differ substantially from the LDM, and, in turn, for the LDM to differ substantially from the CDM/BTM regarding entity-relationship layout, which is the case for our pet adoption initiative.

Subdocuments and "unfoldable" documents

As has been observed with the popularity of single-endpoint GraphQL Web APIs versus multi-endpoint granular-resource-oriented REST APIs, there is often a benefit to optimizing the developer experience so that much of the "glue" work of merging responses to requests for related resources is done server-side rather than client-side.

In TerminusDB, one knob for tuning this is in designating certain classes of documents as subdocuments, which act as "owned" traits of referring documents. Thus, if document A refers to subdocument B and document A is fetched, B is too as a nested subdocument. Furthermore, if A were removed from the database, B would be removed as well.

One may also designate a class of documents as unfoldable. If class B in our previous example was @unfoldable and not a @subdocument, then B would be fetched when A is fetched, but B is also a top-level class, with potentially many referring classes, and so an instance of B would not be transitively removed when an instance of A is removed.

In our initiative's PDM, we made several classes unfoldable to ease validation of Pet documents. Since Pet documents are not too large, it's feasible to fetch and inspect the whole of a Pet's information at a glance.

Git-like collaboration features

TerminusDB uses immutable data structures and delta encoding. Just like how git saves codebase changes by adding and removing lines across files, TerminusDB saves database changes as the assertion and retraction of triples across graphs. That is, as transactional commits with author and intent (aka "commit message") provenance. Furthermore, a TerminusDB database has separate schema and instance-data graphs that are co-validated on every commit to either. Finally, TerminusDB facilitates concomitant workflows for database branching, rollback, time travel to the past (What was the case for the database as of a past commit?), the future (What would be the case for a hypothetical database that includes a candidate commit?), and change requests (aka "pull requests").

We imagine that, for our initiative, the ability of consortium staff to track changes and contributions of adoptable-pet information from the various animal shelters at the database level, including inevitable changes to the schema as new needs are identified, was part of the reason why TerminusDB was chosen.

Compact in-memory representation

Because retrieval from memory is so much faster than retrieval from disk (even from a local SSD or NVMe drive), much less from over a network connection, it's best to have all of a database's information in memory if possible. This is feasible for very small databases, such as for our initiative. However, succinct data structures[5] for compact in-memory representation makes a given hardware budget go farther for an initiative that has a growing database, especially to support graph-oriented queries that may often traverse large and unpredictable swaths of the database. Simply maintaining a table of triples of 64-bit

---

[5] https://en.wikipedia.org/wiki/Succinct_data_structure.

numbers as identifiers would be 24 bytes per triple, whereas TerminusDB can reach under 14 bytes per triple.[6]

Sharding via data products

Sometimes, of course, a database cannot fit in the main memory of a single machine.[7] Many databases have a built-in solution for sharding data across machines for scatter-gather/map-reduce querying within a single logical database. In TerminusDB, the nascent concept of the "data mesh"[8] is the preferred logical container for a domain of data, with various databases conceptualized as so-called "data products" within and part of the mesh. This approach to data organization is useful in collaborative contexts, where each mesh member governs its own database but with the explicit aim of interoperability among member databases.

TerminusDB reifies this notion somewhat via declaring schema classes as Foreign, allowing database integrity to be maintained while excepting references to instances of

---

[6] https://terminusdb.com/blog/big-graph/.

[7] But one can go far, even with pay-as-you-go public cloud instances. At the time of writing (August 2023), Amazon AWS EC2 instances with up to 12TB RAM are available.

[8] Zhamak Dehghani, "How to Move Beyond a Monolithic Data Lake to a Distributed Data Mesh," May 2019. https://martinfowler.com/articles/data-monolith-to-mesh.html.

"foreign" classes, which are proper classes of different TerminusDB databases. The consortium of our initiative plans to keep things simple at first and have a single database with a single schema that members like our shelter will clone, pull updates from, and push branches to, in order to be merged as change requests. However, if certain shelters want to have their own databases while still retaining interoperability with that of the consortium and other members' databases, a data mesh approach with Foreign class references may make sense.

First-class relationships

Many relationships are modeled as attributes of an entity, where there is a natural subject and object of the relationship. For example, in our initiative, a relationship exists logically, such as in our LDM between a Pet and an Image through an attribute of the Pet. This is physically modeled in our PDM as the images property of the Pet class. A Pet is the subject, and a Pet "has" images. However, what if it turns out that a many-to-many relationship is desired because our shelter has many volunteers taking action shots of pets during playtime and wants to use a computer vision tool to tag any pets it can identify in each image?

Conceptually, we may wish to have a PetImageTagging class that relates a pet, an image, and metadata such as confidence score and tool version. Unlike in other database systems, this reconceptualization will incur no performance penalty, just a need to reformulate the application-level queries needed to retrieve and format the desired information. This seems reasonable, as the logical and physical models are kept in alignment with the conceptual model. Said another way, with first-class relationships, a TerminusDB PDM can look an awful lot like a simple expansion of the LDM, which in turn can be a simple expansion of the CDM/BTM.

Multiple inheritance / "mixins"

TerminusDB allows multiple inheritance of classes, resembling ideas such as "mixins", aspect orientation, and traits from programming. This is powerful because optimizations may be done on such traits / mixin classes without requiring any migration(s) of the larger class(es). That is, an optimization, whether conceptual or performance-related, can be a more surgical intervention. Schema evolution is to be expected for any long-term initiative, so the ability to drill down to a more granular level for schema definition and evolution is a benefit.

Collection-valued property ranges

Some document-oriented databases take their cue from JSON and have only objects (maps, dictionaries, (sub)documents) and arrays (random-access ordered collections) as first-class collection-values. In many cases though, a collection-value may be thought of conceptually as a list. That is, as a thing you may iterate through to collect elements but for which you do not expect random efficient access to individual elements by position. This can be especially helpful in situations where a sequence of values can grow "without bound". Without a list type, you may need to worry about whether to "embed" a conceptual list within a parent document. That is, to effectively implement a virtual link structure on top of a database's native document/collection modeling capabilities, etc. In TerminusDB, you can have a List. You can also have an Array that facilitates random access, without worrying about embedding versus referencing.

In other cases, with collection-values, you don't care about ordering. Instead, you may care about cardinality. For example, there being "at least one" of something. In TerminusDB, both can be done natively, and this was how we were able to map the Pet-Image and Pet-Breed relationships from our conceptual BTM diagram and term definitions through to our TerminusDB PDM without much loss. A Pet is assigned a set of Pet Breed instances and is assigned at least one. Furthermore, a Pet is assigned a set of Image instances and is assigned at least one.

Three tips

1. **Workload analysis:** estimates of volume and velocity of access patterns have a major impact on your choice of schema design patterns. And it may evolve over time, requiring to sometimes refactor the schema and corresponding application code. It's often best to treat certain content as binary (large) objects, aka *blobs*, store them and retrieve them from an S3-compatible object store, and include only their identifying URI in the database proper.

2. **Schema versioning and migration:** it is not a matter of if your schema will evolve, but when. Changing customer needs, new strategic direction, unforeseen requirements, scope creep, continuous enhancements, iterative development, etc. It is a fact of life that your schema design will evolve over time. So, you might as well organize yourself for that. TerminusDB has several built-in operations to express and document schema migrations explicitly (*ExpandEnum, UpcastClassProperty,* etc.), as well as handy *JSON Diff and Patch* utilities for document-oriented data migration.

3. **CQRS is for data, too:** Command-Query Responsibility Segregation (CQRS) works well in concert with the Repository and Unit of Work

patterns for persistent storage.[9] This means it is a good idea to leverage features of a database that allow it to be a trusted data repository service that performs units of work with solid transactional guarantees. In other words, move as much logic into the database and out of application-level code as possible. With TerminusDB, leverage the native document orientation, subdocuments/unfoldable-ness, git-like collaboration features over the schema and instance graphs in concert, collection-valued property ranges, etc. For reading data, you have many options as well, from document-oriented retrieval via JSON filter specifications to graph-oriented retrieval via a native datalog (serialized as JSON-LD), to GraphQL (built into TerminusDB).

Three takeaways

1. **Data modeling is flexible in TerminusDB, with comparatively little impact on performance:** Focus on the information gathered and resultant modeling done in the Align and Refine phases, as those models can

---

[9] Percival, Harry J. W., and Robert G. Gregory. Architecture Patterns with Python: Enabling Test-Driven Development, Domain-Driven Design, and Event-Driven Microservices. First edition. O'Reilly, 2020.

often be realized without much refactoring in the Design phase for TerminusDB to achieve acceptable performance, when compared to refactoring needed for database systems that are primarily document-oriented or graph-oriented (or table-row-oriented, for that matter).

2. **Gather knowledge and experience from different stakeholders and domain experts:** developers might be tempted to design schemas all by themselves. There's no doubt that they possess the technical knowledge to design a schema for a JSON document. But to avoid rework of the application code, it is more efficient to first understand the different constraints based on the analysis of the access patterns, the workload, the application flow, and the screen wireframes. Using a diagramming tool facilitates the conversation with non-technical stakeholders and helps reduce the time-to-market of application development efforts.

3. **Data tends to outlive applications by a wide margin:** it might be tempting to think that application code is where schemas are documented and quality is enforced. But data is probably shared by multiple applications. In addition, the lifespan of applications is much shorter than for data. Hence, it is critical to ensure a shared understanding of the meaning and context of data beyond a single application. Data

modeling and schema design for TerminusDB helps achieve this objective. Furthermore, a TerminusDB database can programmatically retrieve schema definitions/documentation (look up the "get class frame" endpoint) as naturally as retrieving instance data. Also, quality is enforced somewhat by every candidate transaction being subject to a full integrity check, including referential integrity, against the hypothetical database-to-be if the transaction succeeds.

Index

www.ingramcontent.com/pod-product-compliance
Lightning Source LLC
Chambersburg PA
CBHW071249050326
40690CB00011B/2327